DOG NUTRITION AND COOKBOOK

THE SIMPLE GUIDE TO KEEPING YOUR DOG HAPPY
AND HEALTHY

THE WOOF BROTHERS

A D

www.publishing.admore-marketing.com

CONTENTS

FOREWORD

Hi, we are The Woof Brothers.

We are a group started by siblings, and our purpose is to help you in all aspects of raising, training, and enjoying the company of your four legged best friend(s).

You may have grabbed this book because you just adopted or bought a new doggy bundle of joy.

Perhaps you are looking for some help with caring for your new canine roommate.

Maybe you have an energy filled teenager who jumps, chews, and leash pulls...

... Or you simply want to get more information on how you can better feed your guy or gal.

Whatever the reason, **we thank you for reading and checking this book out.**

This book is dedicated entirely to teaching you what our group has learned, and helping you have the best relationship possible with your dog. No fluff, just real techniques, that really work.

OUR STORY

There is something about dogs' unconditional love and loyalty that makes people crazy about them. That is how it started for us at The Woof Brothers.

Dogs have saved our lives and taught us more about ourselves than any of the training we raised on to them.

The Woof Brothers consists of not only trainers, but overall dog lovers, and pet owners, who combined all their knowledge to help pass it on to others.

We hope our work helps dog owners achieve a better understanding of their four legged friends and helps lessen the abandonment of dogs, which sadly happens more and more. We believe that if we all took some of the lessons dogs teach us the world would be a better place.

So let's be more like our dog today and live in the moment, not be spiteful, hold no grudges, and see no ethnicity or race.

To find out more and stay updated on our future releases follow our publisher -

- Facebook: facebook.com/admorepublishing
- Instagram: instagram.com/admore.publishing
- Youtube: Admore Publishing

INTRODUCTION

DOGS DESERVE BETTER

Next to your love, affection, and attention, the most pressing concern in your dog's life is a primary and understandable one: food. It's no wonder that your dog comes running the instant she hears you pour food in her bowl or open a package of treats. After all, it's written into the genetics of every domesticated dog, your pup included.

Thousands of years ago, gray wolves and dogs split from an extinct wolf species, and the result was the first of a series of domestications that created one of the greatest relationships in the world: man and dog. Today, your dog may beg for treats, race to her bowl for food, or longingly watch you eat every bite of your dinner, just as her ancestors did millennia ago. Your dog is your companion during mealtimes because that is how humans first developed a friendship with canines, through the bond of food.

As a responsible and loving dog owner, you always want what is best for your pup, and that includes the food she eats. But how do you know what is the right food for your dog? Walk into any pet store, and you'll be greeted with wall-to-wall aisles of every type of dog food imaginable. It can be a frustrating and overwhelming experience if you don't know what kind of food to purchase. Throw in some less than truthful commercial packaging, and it can be downright impossible to tell if what you are feeding your dog is good for her.

Your dog is family, and she deserves better than cheap, processed food that lacks the nutritional value her body and mind needs. By learning about dog nutrition and how to make home cooked food for your pup, you can make sure that your dog gets what she deserves: all the necessary proteins, vitamins, and minerals to eat healthy food and live her best dog life.

What's The Right Food For Your Dog?

To find the best diet for your dog, just pick one bag out of the many sold in pet supply stores that sounds and looks good, right? Unfortunately, that's not the best method to use to select the right food for your dog. Commercial food, both dry kibble and wet, can seem appealing with carefully crafted advertising that claims these foods are "grain-free," "low-fat," or "low-carb." The food may even look attractive to the pet owner, and because you consider your dog family, you want to give them food that looks good to you, rather than thinking of food from the dog's perspective. In truth, your dog could care less about what her food looks like! She just cares about the smell and the taste. That means that the nutritional content is up to you, her owner, friend, and protector.

Many commercial dog foods are packed with artificial ingredients, sweeteners, fillers, and by-products, which provide little to no nutritional value; some, in fact, may cause health problems later in life. These processed diets lack the optimum level of nutrients that canines need, primarily proteins, fats, carbohydrates, vitamins, and minerals. Although these foods may be convenient and cheap, the cost may be high in regards to your pup's current and future health.

The best solution to the doggie diet dilemma is a fresh food diet, either store-bought or homemade. Fresh food diets are formulated with the proper balance of nutrients that your dog needs to be as happy and healthy as possible. Although it is possible to find commercial fresh and raw foods, that still doesn't give you the peace of mind of knowing exactly what is in your dog's diet. By cooking homemade fresh meals for your dog, you can know precisely what goes into each bowl and every treat.

A fresh food diet will have real ingredients as opposed to processed fillers and sugars. Feeding fresh meals to your dog means that she will get the full benefit of nutrients, healthy fats, and antioxidants that her wolf and wild dog ancestors derived from their natural meals thousands of years ago. Commercially produced foods can't offer the same value or nutrition. Those nutritional components are often lost in the cooking process that occurs with dry kibble foods and have been altered from their original fresh state for the sake of lower costs and longer shelf life. You may pay less for the food, and it may last longer in your pantry, but you're robbing your dog of the proteins, carbohydrates, and fats that will make and keep her healthy.

It's In Your Dog's Best Interest

You love your dog like you would your child, and that's why you're reading this book in the first place. As a responsible owner, if you want your dog to eat well and be healthy, consider a fresh, home cooked diet for her sake. Organic, wholesome ingredients and naturally based sweeteners make fresh food highly attractive to your dogs. Once your pup starts eating a homemade diet, you will notice her moving even faster to the kitchen when you are placing her food in her bowl. Not only is this kind of diet better for her, but it will be tastier, too.

Above all, a diet that is full of fresh, wholesome, balanced nutrition will help your dog in terms of her current and future health. Commercialized foods are often full of artificial additives that are not natural to your dog's digestive system; sadly, some of these additives can lead to significant and life-threatening health problems. Fresh foods provide all the protein, fat, minerals, and vitamins that your pup needs for a stronger immune system. The right diet can improve your dog's health now and also help to prevent degenerative, debilitating, and deadly diseases in the future. That will save you money in veterinary bills, but more importantly, it will mean your dog is at your side for longer than she might otherwise be growing up on a commercialized dog food diet.

You might be wondering how you can find the time to cook separate meals for your dog. Doesn't homemade cooking take a long time? Isn't it more expensive than buying a bag of food at the grocery store? Won't it be a messy process? How will you know what to do? It's natural to have questions and concerns about learning how to home cook canine food and switching your dog to fresh food. With this helpful book as a guide, you will find preparing healthy food for your dog easier and less expensive than you think. Best of all, you will feel good knowing that your dog is eating the right food for her well-being and future health.

Like you, your dog is healthiest with
fresh, not processed, foods.

-Megan Spurrell from NomNomNow-

WHY DOG NUTRITION MATTERS

Dog nutrition is critically important for your dog's present happiness and comfort but also for the remaining years of her life. What you feed your dog now may impact her later on when age and illness start to affect her quality of life. You love your dog and want her with you as long as possible, and feeding her food that has the nutrients she needs to stay healthy and mobile can make that hope a reality.

How much of an impact can the right diet have on a dog's body? A tremendous one, it turns out. For your dog's cells to be healthy and perform their individual jobs well, they need to be exposed to healthy environmental stimuli, or wholesome, nutrient-dense foods. If your pup consumes a poor quality of food, especially for an extended period, those negative environmental stimuli are introduced to the body. How will your pup's body respond? Her body will try to fight these stimuli, resulting in inflammation and, eventually, disease.

However, if your dog is on a nutritionally appropriate diet, then the food she ingests will prevent inflammation in the body as well as diseases, giving her a better chance at living a long, healthy, happy life. Fresh food is full of functional superfoods that have a beneficial effect on your dog by promoting healing and reduce chronic inflammation, are powerfully antioxidant, and may even delay the effects of aging.

The Problems With Commercial Pet Foods

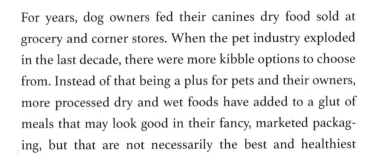

For years, dog owners fed their canines dry food sold at grocery and corner stores. When the pet industry exploded in the last decade, there were more kibble options to choose from. Instead of that being a plus for pets and their owners, more processed dry and wet foods have added to a glut of meals that may look good in their fancy, marketed packaging, but that are not necessarily the best and healthiest option for every dog.

Unfortunately, just as humans have switched from healthy, natural, and traditional diets to quick, processed, and mass-produced foods, we have made the same choices on behalf of our dogs. In a high-pressure, fast-paced society where extra time is a rare commodity, many pet owners choose the convenience of dry kibble which is typically less expensive than high-end foods and available in bulk quantities that last for weeks.

Despite the ease with which kibble is available and its popularity amongst many pet owners, it is not the best option for your dog. There are reasons why the change in the human diet has caused higher rates of degenerative and chronic diseases; sadly, the shift from natural food to a processed one has caused the same results in our pets.

Think of your dog's dry kibble as a version of doggy "fast food." Would you want your dog eating fast food burgers and fries every day? Definitely not! A canine who eats this heavily processed food regularly for years on end is going to develop the same kinds of illnesses that a human being would if they ate burgers and fries daily. Also, feeding your dog the same food all the time limits her nutritional intake. Just as people need variety in their diet, so do dogs. After all, wouldn't you get tired of having spaghetti as your only meal for years on end? Why would you expect the feeling to be different for your dog? Yes, changing up your dog's diet too quickly can cause gastrointestinal upset, but feeding your dog the same thing over and over will lead to more serious digestive diseases in the future.

Another problem with the convenience of dry kibble is that the food quickly loses any nutritional value that it may contain. Kibble may contain the bare minimum of basic canine nutrition, but it doesn't stay that way for long. First, the process of creating kibble in a factory requires multiple rounds of cooking at extremely high temperatures. In that environment, much of the nutritional value of the food is lost. To replace lost nutrition, some food manufacturers spray a nutrient mix and a palatability enhancer to make the food appealing to dogs.

Finally, the concept of any kind of "complete and balanced" kibble is a myth. Once you open a bag of kibble, any nutrients inside of it start to degrade and go rancid. You may think that dry food with a long shelf life is ideal for your pocketbook and your dog's palate, but in fact, it's not. The nutrient mix sprayed on dry food contains sulfates and metal oxides that speed up the oxidation of fats in the kibble, causing them to go bad slowly. Kibble can also be a breeding ground for mycotoxins (toxic chemical substances) and bacteria. Additionally., storage mites, which originate in grain silos, can find their way into kibble food bags. Some dogs are hypersensitive toward these mites and can have allergic reactions to them that may take the form of recurrent ear infections, chronic itchy and inflamed skin, and hair loss.

What exactly are the products in commercial kibble that are potentially harmful to dogs? Here is a sampling of what might be inside of your dog's kibble:

. . .

Poor Quality Meat and Feed-Grade

Poor quality meat and feed-grade ingredients that some pet food manufacturers use in kibble can include meat and bone meal from questionable sources that have been rejected by the human food industry. These sources can be parts of cows judged unfit for human consumption (including the brain, udders, bones, and skin), expired grocery store meat, and in some terrible cases, the carcasses of diseased animals.

Excessive Starches

Excessive starches can often be found in kibble that claims to be "grain-free." These diets include too much starch like peas and potatoes which have a too high glycemic index for dogs. Carbohydrates break down sugars, and eventually, this process leads to degenerative conditions like obesity, diabetes, and cancer.

Low-Grade Proteins and Fats

Low-grade proteins and fats used in most kibble create cancerous by-products when processed at high temperatures. The meat and by-products in kibble are typically cooked through four high-temperature processes, and that affects the digestibility and nutrient value of the food.

. . .

Low-Moisture Content

Low-moisture content is a given with any processed dry food. It's also a real problem as this diet fed over time can cause dogs to be excessively thirsty. The heavy carbohydrate load that takes the place of moisture in dry food is a leading cause of obesity in pets.

Artificial Preservatives, Flavors, and Colors

Artificial preservatives, flavors, and colors are often found in lower-quality and low-cost kibble and are problematic ingredients for a variety of reasons. These components are used as pet food additives to preserve the fat in meat ingredients and to make the dog's food look appealing to potential customers. Aside from the fact that your dog's kibble should not be full of bright colors, these additives cause health problems. Here's a quick breakdown:

Butylated Hydroxyanisole (BHA) and Butylated Hydroxytoluene (BHT)

These are both chemicals added to oil fats and designed to preserve odor, food color, and flavor. The ingestion of both BHA and BHT over long periods are linked to cancer.

Tert-Butyl Hydroquinone (TBHQ)

TBHQ is a fat preservative used to increase kibble's shelf

life. TBHQ has been shown to cause damage to cell DNA and to produce pre-cancerous stomach tumors. Prolonged ingestion of TBHQ may lead to the development of cancer.

Propyl Gallate (also called gallic acid or propyl ester)

Propyl Gallate is a fat stabilizer often used in conjunction with BHA and BHT. This additive has been linked to liver and kidney problems, allergies, respiratory illnesses, and cancer.

Ethoxyquin

Ethoxyquin is a chemical pesticide (yes, you read that correctly) that is used in dog food to stabilize the fat in foods that contain fish. It also preserves the flavor and color of kibble. Dogs consuming high amounts of food with ethoxyquin are at a higher risk for hyperthyroidism, kidney and liver diseases, immune system problems, blindness, reproductive issues, and cancer.

Sorbitol

Sorbitol is a synthetic chemical sweetener used in kibble to keep the food's flavor appealing to dogs. This chemical is sweet enough that it can make dogs overeat, leading to obesity. It can also cause oral decay, hypoglycemia, gastrointestinal distress, and arthritis.

These additives are just the tip of the iceberg. How can this happen with dog food? Unfortunately, there is no governmental oversight of the pet food industry which means that what is advertised about kibble may not be remotely true and you may not be purchasing the ideal food that you thought you had bought for your pup.

In just the above examples alone, it's clear that dry kibble food is not in your dog's best interest. What diet is the most nutritionally appropriate for a dog? Dogs need a diet that includes high-quality animal protein, healthy fats and fiber, vitamins and minerals, moisture, and low to no starch content. Although there are some worthy examples of pre-balanced, portioned, commercially available fresh and raw diets, they tend to get pricey fast. With the right knowledge and the dedication to the purpose, you can home cook your dog's food, save yourself some money, and give your dog food that is appropriate for her happiness and health.

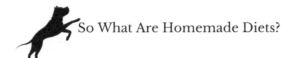 So What Are Homemade Diets?

A home cooked diet is simply a healthy and manageable way to create meals for your dog that are suited to her needs. Ideally, you want to provide as complete and balanced a meal as possible. Check out the general overview for home cooked meal rules here:

- Feed your dog a variety of foods from different nutritional groups.
- Supplement your dog's home cooked diet with calcium if you do not include raw meaty bones in the meal.
- Always stick to lean meats, and remove any skin from chicken to exclude unnecessary fats.
- Review your plan with your veterinarian before you switch your dog onto it.

The preparation of homemade dog food can seem daunting to an owner who has always relied on someone else to make his dog's food, but with careful planning, it's an easier process than you think. In general, here is what you want to have in your variety of home cooked dog meals:

- **Meat and other animal products**
- **Boneless meat**
- **Organs**
- **Fish**
- **Eggs**
- **Dairy**
- **Vegetables**
- **Fruits**

- **Leafy greens**
- **Grains (within reason; see Chapter 2: Nutrition in a Dog's Diet)**

With practice and a set of researched and calculated recipes, you can create your dog's food just as you would when cooking a meal for the rest of your family at dinner. Knowledge and planning are key and make the home cooked process much more manageable.

What Are The Benefits Of Homemade Diets?

A home cooked diet can benefit your dog right now and in the future. Instead of eating biologically inappropriate foods full of questionable meat sources and additives that can cause health problems, your pup can enjoy a freshly cooked meal full of foods that taste better to her than kibble, ingredients that cost less in the long haul, and nutrition that meets your dog's needs. When you consider it from that perspective, wouldn't you want to make the switch for your best four-legged friend? If you're still considering, take a look at these proven benefits to a homemade dog diet.

. . .

More Energy

More energy will have your dog doing zoomies around the backyard no matter her age. Fresh foods are easily digestible, so your dog's body can break down and absorb nutrients faster from that food. Your pup will have more readily available energy to use for walks, hikes, and play at the dog park. Better get those sneakers ready to go!

A Shiny Coat

A shiny coat will make your dog stand out like those fancy pups at dog shows. Homemade diets have healthy essential fats that quickly impact your dog's coat. Within a short week or two, your dog will look ready to strut her stuff at West-minster.

Healthy Skin

Healthy skin means few to no allergic reactions, itchiness, lesions, or other painful and uncomfortable skin conditions. Fresh food has fatty acids, B-complex vitamins, and zinc which are strong anti-inflammatories working to keep your dog's skin clear and healthy.

Bright, Healthy Eyes

Bright, healthy eyes look sparkly on the outside and are well-supported from the inside thanks to a home cooked dog diet. Eye health is one of the first areas of health to suffer as a dog grows older, and feeding a fresh food diet with lots of Vitamin A can help prevent eye health problems from occurring.

A longer, Better Quality of Life

A longer, better quality of life for your pup is something that any good dog owner would sign up for, right? Well, fresh food can offer that chance. So many pet owners have lost their pets to illnesses that may have been instigated by a poor diet. By feeding your dog right, you are buying her extra years at your side.

Less Waste and Firmer Poops...

Less waste and firmer poops... wait, shouldn't every dog owner be lining up for this one? No one is thrilled at having to pick up dog waste off their lawn, and you won't have to do it as often with a dog on a fresh food dog diet. Additionally, the fiber your dog eats is the right kind at an appropriate level. Too much fiber may eventually lead to colon cancer, but on a homemade diet, your dog will eat only the fiber necessary for her health.

A Stronger Immune System

A stronger immune system is developed in dogs who eat healthy, home cooked meals. A wholesome, balanced diet leads to a healthier dog in the present as well as the future as key antioxidants in fresh foods can prevent some diseases and illnesses. The result is that you will have more time with your best friend.

The Quality of Life

The quality of life that your dog has is ultimately what it's all about. You love your dog and want her to be the happiest and most content dog in the world. Well, that also includes giving her food that will supply her with all the nutrition she needs to feel good and live her best dog life.

You Will Save Money

You will save money, full stop. Anyone who owns a pet understands how much their care costs, and trips to the veterinarian's office are typically expensive. Feeding your dog a nutritious and appropriately balanced home cooked diet will prevent future illnesses and save you money you would spend on veterinary bills in the next decade.

Special Dietary Needs

Special dietary needs are easily addressed with fresh food diets. You can create and cook a specialty diet if your dog has food intolerances or sensitivities to certain ingredients. Flexibility is a huge benefit when you are making your own dog food because you can substitute other healthy ingredients for the ones your dog cannot digest.

Control

You have complete control over the ingredients in your dog's food. Unlike any commercial foods which can still leave you wondering what is actually in them, a fresh food, home cooked diet is one that you can serve to your dog with peace of mind because you know every single ingredient in that bowl.

After reading and reviewing these benefits, you might be eager to jump into the world of home cooked canine meals. However, before you make that switch in your dog's diet, there are a few steps to take to make sure you are on the right path.

Before You Make The Switch To Fresh Food...

Transitioning your dog from one food to another is something that shouldn't be done without a conversation with your veterinarian. Make an appointment and talk with the doctor about the dietary change you would like to make and your reasons behind it. Using your dog's current health status and weight along with past veterinary records, your veterinarian can help you devise a home cooked diet with complete meals that covers all the bases of the nutritional levels for your dog.

If your veterinarian is uncertain about fresh food contents and levels, ask for a referral to a board-certified veterinary nutritionist who can develop a diet that is best for your pup. The doctor can tell you want your dog needs nutritionally in terms of age, weight, and breed. Remember that you always have this book as a guide, but it's not a substitute for your veterinarian's medical knowledge of your dog. Don't leave the appointment without having all your questions to the veterinarian answered clearly and thoroughly.

When you are given the go-ahead by your veterinarian, and after you have purchased your ingredients, flip to Chapter 6: Meals to begin reading and trying some of the recipes printed here. All of the meals in this book are designed to be easy to make, highly nutritious, and low-fat. When it's time to consider the process of switching your dog from her old food to the new fresh diet, change your dog's food gradually. Too abrupt a change can cause some unpleasant stomach upset for your pup, including vomiting, diarrhea, and gas.

When making the change, follow these steps to switch your dog over to the home cooked die slowly:

. . .

Gradually Mix The Food

Gradually mix the food by adding a small amount of the new food while slightly reducing the old food; use a 25% new / 75% old ratio to start. Over the next 7 - 10 days, slowly alter the food proportions to a 50% / 50% ratio, then 75% / 25%, and finally, switch your pup over to her new diet entirely.

Keep An Eye Out For An Upset Stomach

Keep an eye out for an upset stomach which can happen during this process even if you are placing your dog on a higher-quality diet. Your dog should be drinking her usual amount of water, she shouldn't have too much gas, and her poop should be firm not runny. Remember to be patient with your dog if she has accidents as her body is adjusting to the new food.

Slow Things Down Even Further

Slow things down even further if you see any uncharacter-istic behavior from your dog such as lethargy or depression. Contact your veterinarian as well for their input on your dog's health status.

. . .

Don't Get Discouraged

Don't get discouraged if your dog doesn't take to the new food right away. Although it's rare, as most dogs will quickly be swayed by the natural smells of fresh dog food, some dogs might turn up their noses at first. They are so used to the kibble they've eaten for so many years that alternatives seem scary. With time, your dog will happily make the leap to fresh, natural food.

If you're thinking that a fresh, homemade food is the right move for your dog, then it's time to go to doggie school to learn some biology in terms of what your dog's body needs to be at her best.

Dogs need a balanced diet that
provides a variety of nutrients. A
healthy diet should be mostly protein
with nutrient-rich vegetables,
complemented by healthy oils and
vitamins.

-Megan Spurrell from NomNomNow-

2

NUTRIENTS IN A DOG'S DIET

Nutrition is critically important to human beings, and it's no different for your best canine friend. Understanding the basics of a dog's nutrition is something that every pet parent should know for their dog's well-being and future health. Many dog owners are not well versed in what and how much dogs should be eating. Their hearts may be in the right place when they choose a food from the store, but if you don't know what's really in the food you're feeding your dog, then you can't be sure it's good for her. Knowledge is power and can be the key to providing your dog with the foundation for a healthy life. Let's take a look at the seven major nutritional classes that make up a well-rounded canine diet.

Proteins

When you watch your dog race around the backyard or leap up in the air to catch a frisbee or tennis ball, she is using her muscles to perform these actions. Those muscles are fueled by proteins which are necessary for healthy tissue and muscle growth. Dogs are capable of making 13 of the 23 amino acids that are the building blocks of proteins; the remaining 10 amino acids must come from your dog's food. Canines require animal proteins in their diet, foods such as meat, poultry, fish, milk, and eggs; these proteins are the easiest ones for your pup to digest.

Canine food may also include vegetable proteins like lentils, beans, and peas; however, these proteins are harder for dogs to digest and don't offer the complete range of amino acids needed for ultimate health. Dog food that combines animal and plant proteins can provide a more comprehensive level of protein content. The amount of protein your dog needs will vary based on her height, weight, age, medical status, and activity level.

 Fats

Do you ever wonder why your dog loves the extra fat from a piece of steak? It's because that fatty slice is incredibly tasty, and for a good reason. Animal fats are a vital part of the canine diet because they are an energy-rich source of calories. They are also carriers for critically important fat-soluble vitamins like Vitamins A, D, E, and K. These vitamins have essential impacts on your dog's body functions (see **Vitamins** below).

Despite the significant role that fats play within the canine diet, too much fat can lead to serious medical issues. Weight gain can easily lead to obesity, which can, in turn, cause cardiac problems, pancreatitis, osteoarthritis and cancer. Remember that fat contains twice as many calories as carbohydrates or proteins, so your pooch's diet should have an appropriate balance between proteins and fats to prevent future diseases instead of causing them.

Essential fatty acids, or EFAs, also play a crucial role in your pup's health. Because dogs can't make these fatty acids on their own, they need to consume a diet that includes EFAs as these fatty acids impact all the cells in the canine body as well as helping to regulate critical body functions. The two most important EFA families are the omega-3s and the omega-6s, and these components strengthen and regulate the immune system, maintain healthy skin and coat, aid in kidney and brain function, and support heart health.

Carbohydrates

Your pup may not need carbohydrates to create energy; after all, proteins and fats can supply a dog with plenty of energy on their own. However, carbohydrates can provide additional fuel for activity and use fiber to keep the gastrointestinal system operating efficiently. The types of fiber that are found in dog food include, potato, oats, whole wheat, and brown rice, although fruits and vegetables also contribute carbohydrates to the mix. Low GI or slow release carbohydrates also help to keep core organs, such as the heart, brain, liver, and thyroid, healthy.

You might be saying, "But what about grains?" After all, stroll down any aisle at a pet food store, and you will see a variety of commercial foods that state they are "grain-free." Does that mean that dogs shouldn't have grain in their diets at all? Actually, dogs benefit from having some grains in their food, but no more than 30 percent of their entire meal. In fact, the U.S. Food and Drug Administration has issued a warning about the potential connections between grain-free dog food and canine dilated cardiomyopathy. Thus, not all grains are created equal, and some are considerably better for your dog, especially if you are going to cook homemade food for her.

Consider these grain bases for your dog's diet:

Buckwheat

Buckwheat contains essential amino acids and rutin, a flavonoid that improves circulation and strengthens the capillaries. This grain neutralizes toxic wastes in the body, improves appetite, and promotes intestinal cleansing.

Millet

Millet is a nutritious cereal grain that is packed with vitamins, minerals, and protein. Because millet is a non-allergenic grain, it is ideal to use for dogs with allergies or sensitive stomachs.

Barley

Barley is a mild cereal grain that has a hearty texture and a sweet flavor. This grain is often used in foods for dogs who are ill, suffering from an upset stomach, or who need to gain weight. Barley contains many nutrients and improves and supports the entire gastrointestinal system and is especially helpful in supporting the thyroid and immune system. Barley include selenium, which prevents the spread of cancer cells.

Oats

Oats contain more protein and fat than most grains. As an adaptogen, oats keep the body in a state of healthy balance by improving its resistance to stress. This grain also regulates the thyroid gland and supports the nervous system. Oats also include beta-glucan, a type of fiber that lowers cholesterol and reduces the risk of heart disease. Because oats are high in fiber, they can have a slight laxative effect on dogs.

Brown and Whole Grain Rice

These are neutral grains that rid the body of toxins and soothe the stomach. Rice may strengthen internal organs as well as support the nervous system. Whole grain rice is an excellent source of B-complex vitamins.

Rye

Rye is a low gluten content grain with a strong flavor to it. This grain helps build muscle, supports bone, nail, and fur formation, and provides energy.

. . .

Teff

Teff is an African cereal grass that is an excellent source of calcium and iron.

Quinoa

Quinoa is the most complete source of protein among plant foods and is an exceptional source of magnesium, iron, phosphorus, and fiber. It contains essential amino acids, including lysine, which is necessary for collagen production. Collagen helps build cartilage, tendons, and ligaments.

What about the most common types of grains such as corn and wheat? These two common grains are often found in processed commercial dog foods. Whereas whole wheat is a nutritious form of wheat, particularly the wheat germ, dry kibble typically includes refined wheat which loses up to 80% of its minerals and vitamins and up to 93% of its fiber. In short, refined wheat and wheat bran are added to commercial dog food as fillers that add some bulk and fiber to the product. Corn is a sugar grain that is used as a filler and which many dogs struggle to digest properly. For these reasons, our fresh food meals do not include these grain sources. For more information about the issues involving these grains, flip to Chapter 5: Foods to avoid and foods to approach with caution.

Vitamins

Just as we need vitamins to power our bodies, your pup needs a proper balance of vitamins to give her the ability to grow, play, and age gracefully and healthily. Vitamins are organic compounds the body needs in certain amounts for metabolic function. There are two categories of vitamins: fat-soluble, meaning they are stored in the liver and fatty tissues, and water-soluble, which are not stored. Vitamins need to come from your dog's diet because her body isn't able to synthesize them in necessary quantities.

Without the proper vitamins at the appropriate levels, your dog's body will not function as it should, leading to a decrease in quality of life for your pup. Here are the vitamins every dog needs in their diet and the food sources they are found in:

Vitamin A

- contains antioxidants that fight disease, promote weight loss, and strengthen skin and eye health.
- Foods that contain Vitamin A: Eggs, fish oil, spinach, carrots, sweet potatoes

Vitamin B-complex

- refers to a variety of Vitamin B sources. Vitamin B1 helps promote normal neurological function and the processing of energy within the body. Vitamin B2 is necessary for energy utilization within cells. Vitamin B12 supports nerve function and biochemical reactions as well as red blood cell production.
- Foods that contain Vitamin B-complex: Beans, green vegetables, whole grains (i.e., teff and brown rice)

Vitamin D

- the "sunshine vitamin," allows the body to balance calcium and phosphorous for strong bones and teeth.
- Foods that contain Vitamin D: Egg yolks, fish oil, cottage cheese, beef

Vitamin E

- is a powerful antioxidant that is essential for fat metabolism and cell function. It also assists with skin and eye health.
- Foods that contain Vitamin E: Whole grains, seeds (such as chia), leafy green vegetables (such as kale)

Vitamin K

- activates your dog's blood clotting abilities and supports bone health.
- Foods that contain Vitamin K: Cabbage, fish, leafy green vegetables

Fiber

Your four-legged best friend needs plenty of fiber in her diet for key physical functions to occur properly. Fiber plays three critical roles in the canine body: digestive health, colon health, and healthy weight maintenance. For digestive purposes, fiber, both the soluble (attracts water) and insoluble (adds bulk) play critical roles in regulating the digestive tract and relieving gastrointestinal conditions such as diarrhea and constipation.

High-fiber food also promotes colon health by fermenting the beneficial bacteria in your dog's intestines and turning it into fatty acids. Those acids then prevent the growth of bad bacteria. Fatty acids can play a role in supporting the recovery of the colon due to injury. Fiber speeds up the digestive and eliminatory processes, which means that waste doesn't sit too long in the intestines. Studies have shown that fermentable fiber may help prevent colon cancer in dogs, so it is a vitally important ingredient in your pup's diet.

If you don't feed your dog correctly, her odds of becoming overweight or obese increase. An overweight dog is one who is more susceptible to developing serious illnesses like heart disease and arthritis. Research estimates that an overweight or obese canine can lose up to two years off of her life, and her quality of life will suffer. A homemade diet that includes appropriate amounts of dietary fibers will make your dog feel full and satisfied without eating as much dry kibble to reach that same point of fullness. Fiber will keep your dog eating only what she should and prevent her from overeating and gaining weight.

Finally, if your dog suffers from diabetes mellitus, a metabolism disorder, she may benefit significantly from a fiber-rich diet. Because fiber slows down the digestive process, blood sugar levels are regulated and prevented from spiking too fast or high. Diabetes mellitus can affect each dog differently, so be sure to discuss adding fiber to your dog's diet with your veterinarian before you do so.

Some excellent examples of foods with dietary fiber that work well in homemade dog meals are sweet potatoes, green beans, and canned pumpkin. Other beneficial sources of fiber can be found in these foods:

- Beet pulp
- Green vegetables

- Apples
- Bananas
- Carrots
- Tomatoes
- Peaches

When transitioning our dog to a fiber-rich diet, proceed slowly. Switching too fast too suddenly will easily cause your pup some unpleasant stomach upset. Slowly substitute small portions of the new fiber-rich food with your dog's current diet, and add a bit more each day until you progress to more of the new food and less of the old. Give your dog's body a few weeks to adjust to the dietary change.

Minerals

As inorganic compounds, minerals are necessary to your dog's everyday body functions. Your pup can't create minerals in her body, so she must obtain them from her diet. The two kinds of minerals, macrominerals and microminerals, are both responsible for a variety of important body functions that are necessary for sustaining life. Here are the minerals your dog needs in her diet and the foods they are found in:

Calcium and Phosphorous

- are key components in muscle growth, nervous system operation, and blood coagulation.
- Foods that contain Calcium and Phosphorous: cauliflower, broccoli, tofu, green beans (calcium); fish, meat, and eggs (phosphorous)
- **Warning:** Too much of these minerals can lead to dangerous side effects including weakness, bone deformities, and bone fractures. Too little causes abnormal development and growth. Puppies need specific amounts of these minerals to foster appropriate and healthy growth.

Sodium, Potassium, and Chloride

- support the balance of cell growth both inside and outside the cells. They also have critical roles to play in the function of the heart, muscles, and nervous system. Stomach acid key to digestion is produced with the assistance of chloride.
- Foods that contain Sodium, Potassium, and Chloride: Vegetables, fruits, grains.
- **Warning:** A disproportion of these minerals may result in dehydration, weakness, hair loss, and in severe cases, paralysis. Abnormal heartbeat is associated with a lack of potassium in the diet.

Iron

- is necessary for the growth and function of red blood cells; it also contributes to enzyme functions, energy production, and a strong immune system.
- Foods that contain Iron: Red meats, poultry, fish, eggs, legumes.

Zinc

- supports protein digestion, strengthens the immune system, and assists cell growth and skin healing.
- Foods Zinc is found in: Liver, eggs, pork, lamb, brewer's yeast

Selenium

- works with Vitamin E to shore up the body's antioxidant defenses and to support immune system health.
- Foods Selenium is found in: Meat, seafood, vegetables, brown rice.

Iodine

- is needed for the production of thyroid hormones for metabolism regulation.
- Foods Iodine is found in: Dairy, kelp, seafood

Manganese

- is necessary for bone development, antioxidant function, and wound healing. Because it is a trace mineral not found as a free element in nature, it is generally found in combination with Iron.
- Foods Manganese is found in: whole grains, salmon, rabbit, beef, eggs, leafy dark vegetables like spinach

Copper

- assists in the formation of red blood cells and the normal growth of tissue and bones. It also promotes the use of Iron.
- Foods Copper is found in: Seafood, seeds, whole grains, legumes

Sulfur

- contributes to the healthy growth of skin, fur, and nails.
- Foods Sulfur is found in: Meat, fish, eggs, molasses

Choline

- plays an important role in neurotransmitter functions, helps to transport fat, and contributes to other critically important reactions in the body.

- Foods Choline is found in: Eggs, meat, fish, liver, soybeans, wheat germ

Magnesium

- supports bone and muscle development and aids in calcium absorption.
- Foods Magnesium is found in: Leafy vegetables, nuts, whole grains
- **Warning:** Magnesium must be balanced in your pup's diet along with phosphorus and calcium. They cannot function properly without each other.

Taurine

- produces bile salts to help the gut absorb fats. It also maintains normal heart health and regulates electrolytes within cells.
- Foods Taurine is found in: Meats, seafood, eggs

At first glance, you might be feeling overwhelmed by this list of minerals and the foods they can be found in. How can you keep track of all of them in your dog's homemade food? Don't start barking up the wrong tree! Talk with your veterinarian about the best ways to cover all your mineral bases in your pup's diet. Then, check out our recipes later on in the book which will make the process much easier for you.

Water

Water is a building block of life for all living creatures, and your sweet dog is no exception to this rule. You might be thinking, "But she has a water bowl filled with fresh water every day. Isn't that enough?" Although fresh water is a necessity for your pup, she also needs to gain water from her diet. Water represents 70 to 80% of an adult dog's lean body mass, and it is necessary for important functions such as: dissolving and transporting nutrients to cells, flushing waste out of the body, supporting the nervous system and organs, regulating body temperature, and hydrolyzing fat, protein, and carbohydrates for digestion.

So how much water does your dog need? That depends entirely on her activity level, her current health, and her environmental temperature. Generally, your pup will self-regulate her water needs, and if she is on a high-moisture diet, she will drink less than dogs who are fed kibble diets. Always make sure that your pup has access to fresh water at all times.

Dogs can eat "people food" (also known as real food)... If you're eating nutritious, whole foods, they're likely the same healthy ingredients your dog should be eating, too.

-Megan Spurrell from NomNomNow-

3

PERFECT PORTION SIZE

So you've decided to feed your dog fresh, homemade meals. How much should your dog eat each day? How much is too much? How much is too little? There are a variety of opinions out in the dog world about portion sizes for dogs, and if you hop online and Google how much you should feed your dog, you will get a million and one answers; many of them may be wrong. All that information can be confusing and overwhelming, and you might find yourself looking longingly at the dry kibble bag in your kitchen cabinet and wondering if this change is really worth it.

Of course it is! After all, this is your pup's health we're talking about. Don't let misinformation prevent you from doing the right thing for your dog. In this chapter, we'll talk about proper portion sizes and give you an idea of what you want to aim for in terms of your dog's diet. Remember, always talk to your veterinarian about the type of food and portion size for your dog before switching diets.

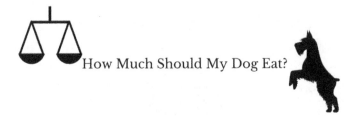

How Much Should My Dog Eat?

The answer to this question is dependent on a variety of variables, including your dog's age and life stage, activity level, and current health and body condition score. That's where your veterinarian can help you tweak the types and amount of food your dog should eat every day. What we can do is provide you with information on the recommended fresh food amounts for dogs of different ages in general.

In general, an adult dog will eat 2.5% of her body weight in raw or fresh dog food daily; large dogs tend to eat lower than that amount while small dogs eat a bit higher than that percentage. If your adult dog weighs in at roughly 31kg, she will need to consume 0.9kg of fresh food each day, or almost 2lbs. For dogs who are younger or senior, and those who are less active or more active, that number will change, sometimes substantially. For puppy feeding amounts, please see Chapter 4: Feeding Growing Puppies.

What Are the Calorie Requirements For An Active Dog?

Perhaps your dog is a working dog who is out by your side in the fields everyday, or maybe she is a breed that is high-energy and requires lots of exercise. How much should she eat if she is an active dog? An active dog should consume a bit more food than an average dog, at least 3% of her body weight. Alternatively, you can feed your pup a higher calorie meal to satisfy this requirement.

How Can I Plan Out My Dog's Meal Contents?

If your dog eats twice a day, divide the total amount of food she receives daily in half for each meal. For an active, leaner dog on the thin side, or for a dog who eats more than she should for her age and size, feed fattier meals first. Alternatively, if your pup is older or less active or is overweight, start the day off with a low-fat meal.

When you are calculating the weight of your dog's meals, don't count any leafy green vegetables as they have so few calories as to not influence the calorie calculations of a dog's diet. Fat content is, however, an important value to plan for and include in your dog's homemade meals. Generally, most dogs need a moderate amount of fat in their diet. As such, you need to limit feeding and foods that have high fat content, which means steering clear of meats that are only 75% lean, and fattier meats like lamb and pork.

To create perfectly portioned meals for your dog, you should follow these three basic rules:

1. Use variety in your dog's meals

Earlier in the book, we talked about how boring eating the same food would be every day of your life. But we also need to acknowledge that consuming one type of food all the time also shortchanges you on nutrition. The same is true for your dog's diet. She needs a variety of foods to provide her with the nutritional standards she needs to stay healthy. Plan to use different meats for the homemade meals you make, such as chicken, turkey, beef, fish, pork, and lamb. Mix in some yogurt, eggs, organs, or other healthy leftovers for additional variety.

If you choose to include grains or vegetables in your meals, remember that the meat and other animal content should make up at least half of the diet, preferably a bit more than that.

. . .

2. Focus on balance in the long-term.

Don't put pressure on yourself to make sure each meal you make is completely balanced in terms of exact nutritional percentages. We generally don't do that with our individual meals, but instead we look at our diet's nutrition as a whole. Apply that same thinking to your dog's diet. Create meals that ensure your dog receives all the appropriate nutrition she needs over the course of a week or two. Think of it as a whole diet approach rather than a day-by-day, meal-by-meal concern.

3. Add calcium when necessary.

People new to feeding home cooked diets often overlook a critically important nutritional component for their dog: calcium. If you are not including bones in your dog's meals, you need to add calcium. What does calcium do for your dog? As we covered in Chapter 2: Nutrients in a Dog's Diet, calcium is a core mineral that is the driving force behind muscle and bone development and growth. This mineral is definitely not one that you want to shortchange your dog on.

Generally, an adult dog needs between 800 and 1,000mg of calcium per pound of food fed. Once you have that down, the calcium content then needs to be balanced in proper proportion to the phosphorus content. Use a calcium:phosphorus ratio in your dog's diet between 1:1 and 2:1. There is a high phosphorus content in meat, so the more meat you have in your dog's diet, the more calcium you will have to add to create an appropriate nutritional balance between these two minerals. Adding the 800 to 1,000mg of calcium will be sufficient even in a high-meat diet, unless you use a calcium supplement that also contains phosphorus. In that situation, you may need to add a higher amount of calcium to balance out the phosphorus.

Where can you find foods with calcium to add to your dog's food? Here are some food item and supplement considerations:

Ground Eggshells:

one large eggshell provides 2,000mg of calcium, so add ½ teaspoon of ground eggshell per pound of food. Do not use eggshells that have been ground into a powder as your pup could have difficulty digesting and absorbing it.

Bone Meal:

this source is often used in diets that don't include raw bones. Be careful though as bone meal includes both calcium and phosphorus. Not all brands of bone meal have the same calcium to phosphorus ratio, and you always want to stick with something between 1:1 and 2:1. Depending on the type of bone meal you use, you may have to adjust the calcium levels to achieve that ratio.

When you purchase bone meal, make sure that the kind you use is free of lead and other contaminants. Avoid using purified bone extracts as too many of these products have high levels of Vitamin D that can harm your dog's health.

Calcium supplements:

Any type of calcium is fine to use in your dog's food in supplement form. Look for calcium supplements that include seaweed, especially as those supplement products typically include other beneficial minerals such as selenium, iodine, and magnesium (see Chapter 2: Nutrients in a Dog's Diet). Remember that most calcium supplements will also include phosphorus, so adjust accordingly to the 1:1 to 2:1 ratio as discussed above.

Use a pre-mix meal:

If the ratios and numbers are making your head swim, or if you are allergic to math, you might find it easier to use a pre-mix meal package. Pre-mix meal packages already have the right amount of calcium and other minerals your dog needs, and all you need to do is add in the meats, eggs, vegetables, and other healthy foods from your homemade meal plan.

. . .

Remember, if you feed your dog meat with ground bone, you do not need to add more calcium to her diet.

Do not feed your dog cooked whole bones unless you have cooked them into a mushy substance via boiling them for hours or using a pressure cooker. Also, although you can cook meals with meat that contain ground bones, too much ground bone will cause your dog some stomach upset like constipation, and in worst case scenarios, impaction. It is best to feed the foods raw or add in an equal amount of meat without the bone to offset the percentage of bone meal in the meal.

What Kinds Of Foods Should I Use For My Dogs Meals?

Your dog's homemade diet needs to include a variety of foods that are fed in appropriate portions. As stated previously, meats, other animal products, eggs, and dairy should make up at least half of the diet, ideally more than that. The overall diet must include both organ and muscle meats, and we'll cover that in more detail below. Here are the types of foods to include and the general amounts to aim for:

. . .

Muscle meat

Muscle meat should be derived from a variety of sources such as beef, chicken, lamb, pork, and turkey. Present the meat in chunks or ground up. Alternatively, you may also feed your dog canned fish like pink salmon, mackerel, or sardines for one or two meals out of the week. A quick note: no calcium supplementation is needed when you feed fish because they include bones.

Kidney and liver

Kidney and liver should represent roughly 5% of your dog's diet, but no more than 10% tops. Feed these meats in small amounts daily or every other day; avoid feeding liver or kidney in large amounts at one time.

Eggs

Eggs provide an excellent source of nutrition, and can be prepared in a variety of ways, such as hard-boiled, soft-boiled, scrambled, or even raw if your pup enjoys them in that form. Feed as many eggs as you like provided that you are still feeding your pup lots of variety.

Dairy products

Dairy products ranging from yogurt to cottage cheese to kefir can offer tasty nutritional value for your dog. Use kefir or yogurt that includes added probiotics for an extra nutritional boost. Probiotics contain beneficial bacteria that will support your dog's gastrointestinal system. Add these products after the meal has been cooked.

Vegetables

Vegetables are optional additions to your dog's diet, but are beneficial in their own right. The best vegetables to feed your dog are leafy greens. Other exceptional additions to consider are broccoli, cauliflower, celery, cucumber, zucchini, bell peppers, brussels sprouts, bok choy, rutabaga, summer squashes, turnips, carrots, and cabbage. You can feed swiss chard and spinach in limited amounts as well.

Steam the vegetables if possible so they don't lose as much of their nutrients as they do when boiled. Feel free to add the water left over after steaming the veggies to your dog's meal as that water still contains some minerals that were drawn out of the vegetables during the steaming process. You can even add gravy, soup, or meat drippings to the water for a tasty broth.

Because vegetables have so few calories, just add them to the top of your dog's cooked meal instead of calculating them as a percentage in your dog's overall diet. Too many vegetables can cause gas in some dogs, so keep them in proportion to the overall meal.

. . .

Grains, starchy vegetables (sweet potatoes, potatoes, winter squash), and legumes (beans)

These are additional options to include in cooked diets. Keep them a small percentage of your dog's diet, about ¼ or less.

Any of the grains listed in Chapter 2: Nutrients in a Dog's Diet are acceptable for homemade cooked meals. Feed a variety of grains just as you would feed a variety of meats. If your dog is overweight or suffers from gastrointestinal disorders such as Irritable Bowel Syndrome, grains might not be appropriate for her diet. If that's the case, talk with your veterinarian first before adding grains to the meals.

Fruits

Fruits may be added to your dog's diet, but only in small amounts. Use fruits such as apples, berries, melons, mangoes, or papaya and keep in mind that overripe fruits are easier for your dog to digest. Do not feed your dog raisins or grapes under any circumstances as these fruits can cause extensive kidney damage, and in dogs with higher sensitivity to these fruits, that damage can happen quickly and become fatal.

When you are cooking your meals, you may find it more convenient to cook up batches of food at one time. This approach allows you to divide the batches into individual, meal-sized portions, and freeze them for later use. Variety is more important to your dog over time than at every meal, so don't be afraid to feed your dog the same food for a week or so. Switch to a different meal when you make the next batch.

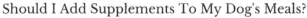

Should I Add Supplements To My Dog's Meals?

Adding supplements to your dog's diet is entirely your decision, though it would be wise to discuss whether they are needed, and if so what kinds, with your veterinarian before adding anything to your dog's food. Here are some supplements to consider adding due to the nutritional value they provide for your pup:

Fish Oil

Fish oil is perhaps the most important supplement to add to your dog's food. Use EPA oil or salmon oil. Fish oil has essential fatty acids such as Omega-3 and Omega-6, which strengthen the immune system and promote healthy skin and coat. Do not use sources with cod liver oil, flaxseed oil, or carmelina oil as these sources are too difficult for a dog's body to process fatty acids from properly.

Minerals

Minerals should ideally be derived from whole foods as supplementing them can be tricky and sometimes dangerous at excessive levels. Aside from calcium supplementation, covered earlier in this chapter, try to use whole food forms like green blends for mineral supplementation. A multi-vitamin and mineral supplement may be feasible for your dog's diet, but get your veterinarian's opinion before feeding any mineral supplement to your dog.

Probiotics

Probiotics are a helpful supplement especially if your dog has stomach or digestive issues or is suffering from illness or stress. Use probiotic supplements that include multiple strains of beneficial bacteria as opposed to plain acidophilus. *Bacillus coagulans* and *Enterococcus faecium* are the two types of bacteria that are most beneficial to dogs. A digestive enzyme might also be appropriate if your dog suffers from long-term gastrointestinal disorders.

Add any supplements that you plan to use to the food right before giving it to your dog. Mixing supplements into the meals ahead of time, and then freezing them, can affect the nutritional value of the supplements. For example, the probiotics in kefir or yogurt will not survive the freezing process, thereby robbing your dog of those beneficial nutrients.

Spices and herbs can be added for more flavor to your dog's meals. Do not include onion or any other member of the onion family in the food as these sources can cause anemia in your dog.

Now you have a wide variety of meal ingredients to choose from. Our next step is to figure out how often your dog should eat her meals, and that means developing a schedule that works for you and your dog.

Setting Up A Feeding Schedule For Your Dog

Dogs live for routine; it provides them a sense of security and safety in their environment. While your dog can't tell time as we do, she does have an internal clock that lets her know when it's time for a routine task to happen. Add in some stomach rumblings and drool, and your dog's body will definitely let her know when it's time to eat, and she will promptly share this information with you!

Similarly to the amount of food your dog should eat, her feeding schedule will also be influenced by her age and activity level. Again, create an exact schedule for your dog with your veterinarian's input and advice based on his or her knowledge of your dog's age and health. Below, we are providing a general schedule that can be modified to suit your dog's individual needs.

The typical adult dog should be fed twice a day to stabilize her metabolism and promote healthy digestion:

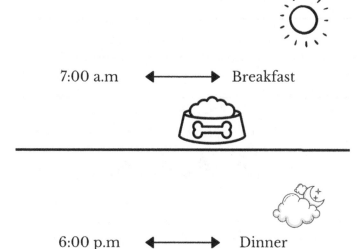

7:00 a.m ⟷ Breakfast

6:00 p.m ⟷ Dinner

Part of developing a schedule for your dog is taking into account other important factors in her day, including when she drinks water and exercises. These parts of the schedule are also important for both digestive and potty break purposes. Here is a general water schedule for an adult dog:

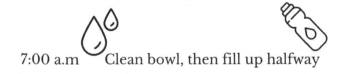

7:00 a.m   Clean bowl, then fill up halfway

12:00 p.m   Rinse out bowl and refill halfway

6:00 p.m   Rinse out bowl and refill halfway

Bedtime   Clean bowl and refill ¼ of the way

Exercise is crucial to your dog's physical and mental health. The proper level of activity for your dog will prompt her to eat her food regularly. A general activity or exercise schedule might look like the following:

6:30 a.m Walk before breakfast (at least 15 minutes)

12:00 p.m Walk (at least 5 minutes)

5:00 p.m Walk before dinner (at least 15 minutes)

These are just model schedules that you can use and modify to work with your schedule. You can change and add to them as you see fit and create a plan that works best for you and your pup.

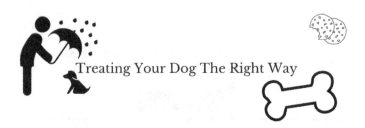

Treating Your Dog The Right Way

We've arrived at the point in the book that your dog is most interested in: treats! Yes, treats can be part of your dog's homemade meals, and we'll even provide some do-approved recipes for you later in the book. But it's important to understand why home cooked treats are just as important as home cooked meals. In this case, it goes beyond just nutritional content; it's also about your dog's safety.

Every year, some commercial treats are recalled for contaminants such as salmonella, melanine, toxic molds, and metal shards. In 2007, hundreds of dogs in the United States suffered from kidney failure due to 5,300 treat products, all imported from China, that were full of contaminants and which were being sold by major pet food companies and stores. Since that time, commercial treats have gradually improved and there are healthier options available on shelves now. However, just because a bag of treats has a "Made in the USA" stamp on it does not mean it's automatically healthy or safe, or even made in that country!

Unfortunately, many of the unhealthy and dangerous options, often the cheaper ones, remain on the shelves. Just in the last two years, the United States Food and Drug Administration (FDA) has received over 5,000 reports of sickness related to pet treats, specifically jerky treats and chicken treats, strips, and tenders. Complaints have also been made about duck jerky treats, treats with dry fruit in them, rawhides, and sweet potato jerky.

You can save your dog the agony of suffering for her treats by making them on your own. Just as with your pup's meals, you will know every ingredient that goes into her treats because you will control the process. Your dog will love her new, yummy, healthy treats, and you will love to give them to her knowing that everything in them is nutritious and safe.

Dogs have about 1,700 taste buds.
Humans have approximately 9,000
and cats have around 473.

-*Psychology Today*-

4

FEEDING GROWING PUPPIES

We've learned about general nutrition for adult dogs, but what happens if you are bringing a puppy into your home? Puppies have a different set of nutritional demands than adult and senior dogs. That adorable fluffy ball of energy who delights in doing zoomies around your coffee table at precisely 8:30PM every night is a growing being who needs more energy and nutrients at this stage of her young life. From day one, your puppy depends on good nutrition not only to power her way through each day, but also to prepare her body for rapid growth into adulthood. Let's take a look at exactly what kind of nutrition your puppy needs for a happy present and a happy future.

Puppy Power, Naturally

All that fun-loving, racing around the backyard, giving lots of kisses energy that your puppy seems to have an endless supply of is actually powered by the food she eats. That diet should be formulated to create the foundation for your puppy's development. Bone, brain, and organ development happen quickly in puppies, and those three components are the key to your puppy having normal body functions both as a puppy now and as a healthy adult dog in a year or so. Young dogs require higher levels of protein, calcium, fats, and phosphorus compared to adult dogs. These facts mean that your puppy must have nutritional balance to grow up healthy and strong. Too much of certain nutrients can cause lifelong health complications while too few nutrients may result in deficiencies. With the proper home cooked diet, you can ensure that your puppy will have every vitamin and mineral she needs as she races around your house and further into your heart.

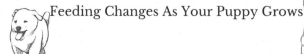Feeding Changes As Your Puppy Grows

Unfortunately, as cute as your puppy is, she won't stay small for long. Puppies develop quickly, with most dogs reaching adulthood by or just before the age of one year; the exception is for extremely large breed dogs, such as Great Danes, who can take upwards of two years to reach adulthood. Proper nutrition is essential as your puppy grows, and because her body has different needs at specific times of that growth, some feeding changes are necessary during her first year of life. Many puppy parents wonder how often to feed their dogs, and we've provided a general feeding schedule for you to follow.

First 3 months:

A puppy's first three months of life are marked by rapid growth. Many puppy parents bring their puppy home after she has been weaned from her mother's milk and has been moved onto solid foods, although puppies can begin eating semi-solid foods at around the 3-week mark.

Because puppies are effective at regulating their food intake fairly well during this early period, you can leave food out to let your puppy graze freely. If you feel that your pup is overeating, then switch to putting the food out at frequent intervals, starting with four times a day.

Months 4 to 6:

At this stage, your puppy can switch to three-a-day feedings; eventually, around months 5 to 6, your puppy will be ready for two-a-day feedings. Your job as a pup parent during these months is to make sure your puppy doesn't overeat and become fat. Puppies in this period will eat quite a bite, generally about twice as much food per pound as an adult dog of comparable weight.

Your chubby puppy might look cute, but extra weight leads to extra medical problems. Large puppies breeds can be especially impacted by being even slightly overweight. Orthopedic bone development issues can occur, and these growth problems will impact your puppy for the rest of her life. Check your puppy's body condition; ideally, you should be able to feel her ribs gently and see a visible tuck in the waist or abdomen from the side and above. If you aren't sure if your puppy's weight is where it should be, whether she is overweight or underweight, take her to the veterinarian for a professional's opinion and advice.

Months 6 to 12:

Most puppies are beginning to approach adulthood at this point, and meals twice a day are appropriate. Depending on your puppy's breed, she may even move to eating adult food during this time; smaller breeds typically complete their growth during this time while larger breed dogs will continue to grow for upwards of another 6 to 12 months. For larger breed puppies, controlling the amount of calcium they receive is critical to their future health.

Months 12 to 18:

By 1-year of age, your puppy isn't really a puppy anymore. From 12 to 18 months, twice daily feeding should be the standard feeding schedule. Unless your dog has slowed down in terms of her daily exercise, this level of feeding is acceptable. For small and medium-sized dogs, it is time to switch to adult nutritional levels in food. Large breed dogs will still have some growing to do for the next year and should still be consuming a diet that provides nutrition levels for puppies.

Development And Changes In Diet

Now that you have a basic puppy feeding schedule to follow, you want to consider what kind and how much fresh food to give your pup. Initially, during the first three months, you want to provide moist foods that are easy for your puppy to mouth, chew, and digest. Water is one of the most important ingredients that your puppy can have in her food during this period. Mashing moist food together with a fork is a simple way to create foods that are tasty and portioned appropriately for your little one.

Similarly to why home cooked foods are better for adult dogs, puppies benefit from a fresh food diet in multiple ways. But what kind and how much are our considerations now. Here are some important factors to keep in mind when preparing fresh food for your puppy.

Fresh Food Calories

Food calories are not all equal. A calorie of fresh food is not the same as a calorie of dry kibble. Fresh food is highly digestible, certainly more so than dry kibble or processed wet foods, so your dog receives more nutrients and energy by eating less volume of food. In other words, you get more puppy power per calorie in fresh food, meaning your puppy doesn't have to eat as much of it as she would dry or wet processed foods to reach the same energy and nutrient levels. How well your pup will digest fresh foods depends on a variety of factors, including cooking methods, quality of ingredients, and amounts of fats, proteins, and carbohydrates.

Most commercially processed food calories are calculated according to animal feed guidelines established by groups like The Association of American Feed Control Officials (AAFCO). The calorie counts in this type of food are what you see on the sides or backs of dog food packages. However, fresh food dog diets should be calculated using a modified factor similar to that used for human foods. The reason for this similarity is due to humans and dogs having similar digestive systems. For dogs on a fresh food diet, proteins and carbs are 4 calories per gram while fat is 9 calories per gram.

Feeding small breed puppies

Select the correct food portion for your small breed puppy based on her predicted adult weight If you aren't sure what her weight might be as an adult, consult your veterinarian who can help. Once you have that information, take the following steps:

Don't go overboard with treats.

- It's hard not to want to give your puppy treats when she behaves, follows commands, or just looks as cute as can be. Treats, especially ones you can purchase at pet or grocery stores, can add far more calories to your puppy's daily diet than you think. Go easy on the treats and on your pup.

Watch those portions.

- Because small breed puppies approach adulthood

faster, their metabolism is likely to slow down more quickly than it does for large breeds. This situation is especially true if you frequently carry your small breed puppy around (yes, we're looking at you!).

Feeding large breed puppies

Like a small breed dog, proper portion sizes for your large breed puppy should be based on her predicted adult weight; again, talk to your veterinarian if you don't have a good idea of your dog's expected adult weight so you can have a definitive number to work with. Here's what to keep in mind when composing food portions for a larger breed:

Watch your puppy's food intake closely.

- As large breed puppies are more susceptible to growth development issues due to imbalanced or poor nutrition, you need to keep a watchful eye on how much your puppy eats and what the nutrient levels are in her fresh food diet. Too many calories and too much calcium may lead to bone growth issues that will impact your puppy for the remainder of her life.

Check your puppy's body condition regularly.

- As stated previously, your puppy's body condition should show a tuck or indentation at the waist from the side and above. You should be able to feel your puppy's ribs when you gently touch her sides. If you are unsure of your dog's body condition level, ask your veterinarian to tell you.

How much fresh food is right for your pup?

Once you have your puppy's predicted adult weight, you can begin to plan for how many calories your dog should consume daily. Our fresh food puppy feeding schedule is a guide for you to use as a reference, but as every dog has individual needs, remember to check with your veterinarian or a board-certified veterinary nutritionist to get the correct amount of daily calories for your puppy.

Puppy's Estimated Adult Weight (lbs)	Daily Fresh Food Calorie Intake
5	192
6	220
7	247
8	273
9	298
10	322
12	369
15	437
18	501
20	542
25	641
30	734

Puppy's Estimated Adult Weight (lbs)		Daily Fresh Food Calorie Intake
35	⟶	824
40	⟶	911
45	⟶	995
50	⟶	1077
55	⟶	1157
60	⟶	1235
65	⟶	1312
70	⟶	1387
75	⟶	1460
80	⟶	1533
85	⟶	1604
90	⟶	1674
100	⟶	1812
110	⟶	1946
120	⟶	2077
130	⟶	2206
140	⟶	2332
150	⟶	2456
170	⟶	2697
190	⟶	2932
210	⟶	3161
230	⟶	3384

Data Source: https://www.nomnomnow.com/puppy-feeding-guide#importance-of-proper-puppy-nutrition

What Does A Balanced Fresh Food Diet For Puppies Look Like?

Because your puppy's diet won't be exactly like any other dog's diet, remember to involve a professional along with using this book to develop your puppy's fresh food menu. You will need to start with a balanced diet that includes protein, carbohydrates, fats, minerals, and vitamins. You will want to add some supplements as well with your veterinarian's guidance and input.

You can follow these basic guidelines for ingredient proportions on the next page:

Ingredient		Portion Percentage	Food Options
Protein	⟶	40 - 80%	Boneless chicken, beef, pork, lamb, turkey, duck, salmon; eggs cooked with crushed shells.
Fats	⟶	5 - 15%	Poultry skin; poultry fat from cooking; soybean, safflower, or canola oil; flax oil or ground flax seeds.
Carbohydrates	⟶	20 - 60%	Regular & sweet potatoes; brown, white, or jasmine rice; lentils & peas; barley & oatmeal in small portions
Vitamins & Minerals	⟶	Vet-recommended %	Discuss what supplements your puppy could benefit from aside from what she will receive from this diet.
Vegetables & Fruits	⟶	5 - 10%	Carrots, peas, berries, etc. See Chapter 5: Foods to Avoid for dangerous fruits & vegetables to steer clear of.
Extras	⟶	Your call	You can save and add broth, soup, or other tasty leftovers.

Data Source: https://www.petcarerx.com/article/making-homemade-puppy-food/1224

Next, it's time to cook the food. Many pet parents who home cook their dog's food find it easier to pick one or two days a month to cook the food in bulk. You can use portion-sized containers to make it easy to feed your pup when mealtime comes. Cooked meals will last about five days in the refrigerator, and up to six months when frozen. This method will help you know well in advance when your supply is running low so you can plan a time to cook another batch. As it is a nutrition-ally sound idea to switch up the type of meal you serve every one to two weeks, you may find color coding with markers or sticky notes to be a good way to keep track of meal types.

Here is a simple process to follow for preparing your puppy's fresh food diet:

1. Place all the ingredients together into a saucepan. Do not include any supplements at this time.
2. Add some water or non-sodium broth.
3. Heat on low to medium heat until everything has been thoroughly cooked.
4. After the ingredients have been cooked, allow them to cool.
5. Once cooled, take the food and mash, chop, shred, or mince the meal. You may choose to use a food processor or blender if that is easier and quicker for you.
6. Break the meal up into proper portions and store

them. Small plastic containers or muffin tins work well for storage purposes.

7. Add any vet-approved supplements into the meal before you serve it; do not put supplements in food that will not be served immediately as those supplements will lose their value if refrigerated or frozen.

As always, speak with your veterinarian on a regular basis as you work through this process. It is vital for you to call your vet if you notice anything unusual in your puppy's behavior, including vomiting, diarrhea, lethargy, bloated abdomen, dizziness, uncoordinated movements, or pale or blue gums.

By following these steps, and using the recipes located in Chapter 6: Meals, your puppy will be on her way to proper growth and development while eating tasty home cooked meals prepared by her favorite person: you!

Puppies have 28 teeth and normal adult dogs have 42.

-about.com-

5

FOODS TO AVOID AND FOODS TO APPROACH WITH CAUTION

Hopefully, you're feeling empowered enough to begin cooking homemade food for your dog. Before you start, however, there are some foods you need to know about that can be dangerous or potentially threatening to your pup. These are foods that you never want to include in your cooked meals, and ideally, keep out of the reach of your dog even outside of her meals. We've compiled a list of dangerous foods to avoid as well as why they are problematic and even fatal if your dog ingests them.

This Or That? Yes Or No?

If you take a moment to look up "foods dogs should avoid" in an internet search, it won't be a surprise if you find yourself quickly overwhelmed with a multitude of different responses. Some sources will say this food or that one is dangerous, or potentially fatal to canines; others will state that those foods may be bad only in certain circumstances. What's a concerned dog owner to do? First, check with your veterinarian about any foods you have questions about before you begin cooking. Then, use our handy guide now and in the future to double check any foods with which you may have continued concerns.

Foods To Avoid

Not all human foods are dangerous for dogs; after all, you are going to use human-grade foods when you make home cooked meals for your pup. But it is important to understand which human foods are toxic to your dog so you can create safe meals in a safe environment for her. These are foods dogs should steer clear of at all costs:

. . .

Alcohol

Alcohol can have a significant impact on a dog's health, even in small doses. It is far more toxic to canines than it is to human beings. Do not feed your dog any alcoholic beverages or foods with alcohol in them, such as pure or artificial extracts, liquor-flavored desserts, pastries and cakes, cooking spray, wine-flavored cheeses, malt or wine vinegars, and cooking wines.

Effects: Dogs who ingest alcohol may cause central nervous system depression, vomiting, inhibited motor function, coma, and death.

Almonds

Although almonds are not toxic in dogs like many other members of the nut family, their size makes them a safety threat if they are not chewed thoroughly and completely. If you know dogs, you know that chewing thoroughly and completely is not their forte, so keep almonds far away from your dog.

Effects: Almonds can easily tear the windpipe if they are not chewed completely. They may also block the esophagus, leading to choking or difficulty breathing. Salted almonds can cause water retention which can be fatal to dogs with heart disease.

Avocado

Avocado has a substance called persin in its seeds, leaves, skin, and fruit, Even small amounts of avocado can cause a reaction in dogs.

Effects: The symptoms of avocado toxicity are diarrhea and vomiting.

Blue cheese

As with other dairy products, dogs cannot easily digest cheese, and higher fat varieties pose particular challenges to the canine digestive system. Blue cheese is an especial problem for dogs because it contains stilton and roquefort cheese. Some dogs are highly sensitive to roquefortine C, which is used in many blue cheese.

Effects: Ingesting roquefortine C may cause dogs to vomit or have diarrhea. In large overdoses, dogs may also have tremors, seizures, and fever.

Caffeine

As with chocolate, caffeine of any kind, including coffee and tea, is not safe for dogs to consume because it is a stimulant. The ban on caffeine covers all forms such as coffee beans, coffee grounds, brewed coffee, and tea leaves.

Effects: Caffeine ingestion results in a rapid heartbeat, diarrhea, vomiting, hypertension, seizures, and death.

. . .

Cherries

Although the cherry pulp is no danger to a dog, the pit within the cherry is a health issue. Cherry pits contain cyanide, a toxic chemical compound. Keep all cherries and discarded pits away from your dog at all times.

Effects: If a dog eats enough cherry pits, and for some dogs that could be a few and for others a whole bowl or two, she can experience any of the following: difficulty breathing, bowel blockages, and death.

Chocolate

It might be a sweet treat for people, but chocolate is definitely not a safe food for canines. Chocolate has theobromine, a compound primary alkaloid that gives chocolate its mood-altering effects. While that may work in your favor after a rough day at work, it is toxic for your dog. Theobromine is a member of the methylxanthine family, which also includes caffeine and other stimulants. Dark chocolate has the highest concentration of theobromine, and thus is more dangerous than milk chocolate or white chocolate.

Effects: If your dog ingests chocolate, she may suffer from vomiting, diarrhea, seizures, high blood pressure, excessive panting, kidney failure, and even death.

Cooked bones

Under supervision, it is fine for a dog to chew on a raw bone. It is not safe, however, to let your dog have a cooked bone. They can too easily splinter and break.

Effects: If your dog gets ahold of a cooked bone and eats it, she may suffer from constipation in a best case scenario. In worst case situations, your pup may choke on the bone, develop an intestinal obstruction, damage her teeth while chewing it, or the bone splinters can cause internal damage such as a perforated gut.

Corn on the cob

In this case, it's not the corn that is the issue; it's the cob. If you want to feed your dog corn, do it off the cob. The cob itself can break off and is difficult for dogs to digest.

Effects: The cob is a choking hazard, and it may also cause blockages in the gastrointestinal system. Blockages need immediate surgery to remedy the problem, otherwise, death can occur.

Garlic, onions, and chives

All members of the onion family are dangerously toxic to dogs in any form, including dehydrated onions, onion slices, raw onions, cooked onions, and any food or table scraps that include onions, garlic, or chives. These vegetables and herbs should never be included in your dogs home cooked meals. Onions, chives, and garlic can typically be found in pizza, commercial baby foods, takeout meals, and condiments such as sauces and gravies (these may contain garlic or onion powder).

Effects: A dog ingesting onions, garlic, or chives may suffer a range of issues from stomach upset and other gastrointestinal issues to red blood cell damage and anemia. These symptoms are likely to show up over an extended period of time as opposed to right away.

Grapes and raisins

Although the exact reason is unknown, grapes and raisins are toxic to dogs. Small amounts can cause severe reactions in some dogs, and that's a chance you don't want to take with your pup. Remember, these fruits are not only dangerous in their original form, but also when they are used in other foods, especially raisins which can be found in cereals, biscuits, muffins, and cakes.

Effects: For some dogs, even a tiny amount of grapes or raisins can result in sudden kidney failure. Many dogs will experience severe kidney or liver damage, which, in some cases, can be fatal long term.

Immature regular or sweet potatoes or tomatoes

While mature, fully grown potatoes and tomatoes are perfectly fine for your dog to consume in proper portions, immature plants are a danger. While growing, the stem, skin, and leaves of the potato and tomato are full of sola-nine, a defensive poison. If a dog eats enough immature potatoes, serious health issues can occur. If there is any green on the tomato or potato you are planning on giving to your dog, hold off until it is fully ripened and no longer immature.

Effects: Consuming too much solanine can lead to nervous system damage, blurred vision, slowed heart rate, and upset stomach.

Macadamia nuts

No one knows the exact toxin that makes macadamia nuts so deadly to dogs; they just know that dogs will suffer if they ingest them, even in tiny amounts. Macadamia nuts, or desserts that include them, such as chocolate, cookies, and ice creams need to be out of your pup's reach at all times.

Effects: It takes as little as 12 hours after ingestion for symp-toms of macadamia nut poisoning to appear in a dog, including hind end weakness, vomiting, depression, swollen limbs, tremors, excessive panting, and fever.

Milk

Dogs don't have enough of the lactase enzyme to break down milk or milk products efficiently. If possible, avoid giving your dog any dairy products that include milk.

Effects: A dog who consumes milk or milk products may develop gastrointestinal issues such as diarrhea or vomiting.

Moldy foods

You typically throw away foods that have become moldy; just make sure you toss them in a garbage your dog can't get into. Moldy foods like bread and dairy products contain fungal neurotoxins that can harm your dog if she eats them.

Effects: The side effects of a dog eating moldy foods range from vomiting and diarrhea to tremors, seizures, and fever. These symptoms may occur from 24 to 48 hours, and if left untreated, can be fatal.

Mushrooms

There are a hundreds of mushroom plants, and only 100 of them are poisonous. The trick is trying to identify the ones that are and aren't deadly, which can be tough to do if you are not an expert on the subject. Generally, it is best to avoid feeding mushrooms to your dogs and to not let her eat any wild mushrooms she may encounter while outside. Cooked mushrooms may have onion or garlic powders or sauces with xylitol, all of which can be fatal for a dog in the worst circumstances.

Effects: A dog who consumes a mushroom that is either poisoned or that she has a sensitivity to may exhibit these symptoms: lethargy, uncoordinated movements, excessive drooling, stomach pains, diarrhea, vomiting, seizures, and tremors. Left untreated or in extreme cases, a dog may suffer kidney failure, liver disease or failure, coma, and death.

Plums

As with cherry pits, plum pits are the concerning factor with this fruit. Plum pits also contain cyanide, and a dog who eats some plum pits is a dog headed for some medical trouble.

Effects: Like cherry pits, the ingestion of plum pits can cause a dog to suffer from bowel blockages, difficulty breathing, and death.

Salt

As people, we love to add salt to just about everything we eat; in fact, most of our processed foods already include more salt than we need. Our dogs don't require the same levels of salt that we do, and if a dog eats foods that are high in salt content, she will likely suffer for it. Don't add salt to your pup's cooked meals and keep salty foods, especially snack foods, far away from inquiring noses that would like to share some potato chips with you.

Effects: Excess salt consumption leads to high blood pressure, heart problems, and kidney dysfunctions.

Walnuts

Walnuts are hard for many dogs to digest, resulting in a host of stomach and digestive problems. These nuts take a long time to be broken down by the digestive system, and because they are high in fats, they can cause some nasty stomach aches for your pup.

Effects: Walnuts can be choking hazards and can cause bowel obstructions. Avoid feeding them to your dog.

Xylitol (artificial sweeteners)

A common additive, xylitol is an artificial sweetener often found in sugar-free foods. It is categorized as a sugar alcohol, and may be included in foods such as peanut butter, baked goods, pudding snacks, and candies. It is also in some cough syrups, chewable and gummy vitamins, nasal sprays, laxatives, and human prescription medications amongst other items, so it's best to make sure your dog cannot reach any of these sources if they are in your home.

Effects: Xylitol can cause low blood sugar (hypoglycemia) and liver failure in dogs because of its impact on insulin regulation in the body. Symptoms of xylitol poisoning are fatigue, loss of coordination, and vomiting.

Yeast

Dogs who ingest unbaked bread place themselves in real danger. When eaten, the yeast in the dough expands within the stomach, quickly resulting in stomach distension and, in dire circumstances, bloat. Additionally, when the yeast uses sugars in the fermentation process, it creates alcohol and carbon dioxide which are released into a dog's bloodstream. Ingestion of alcohol by any means can be fatal to a dog.

Effects: Dogs who ingest yeast may experience a distended stomach, bloat (gastric dilation-volvulus), dry heaving, vomiting, alcohol poisoning, elevated heart rate, weakness, collapse, and death.

Keep this list of foods that your dog should never consume close at hand. If you see your dog eat one of these items, or you think she might have done so, call your veterinarian right away or contact your local or national poison control center. Use this opportunity to get educated about what foods to keep away from your dog and to get motivated about cleaning your kitchen to make sure no harmful foods are within reach of your puppy's mouth.

Foods To Be Cautious With

Some foods are not necessarily dangerous to dogs, but they should only be fed to canines with extreme caution. Not all dogs react to the same food in the same manner; just as humans can be allergic to some foods, dogs can as well. Trial and error is all fine and well, but you don't want to play around with your dogs health and well-being. Here are some foods to approach with caution before including them in your dog's diet.

Apples

While the apple fruit is fine in small doses, the apple seeds are not as they contain cyanide. Also, apple cores are a serious choking hazard. Only feed sliced, unseeded apples to your pup.

Apricots

Like apples, the apricot fruit is safe for a dog to eat; however, the seeds are a danger. Apricot seeds contain cyanide, and the pit is the right size to be swallowed whole and cause a choking hazard or blockage.

Bread

Small amounts of bread are fine for your dog to consume provided the bread is plain without butter, spices, added sugars, or raisins. However, bread does not have nutritional value for pups, and just takes up carbohydrate calories that could be better spent. Homemade breads are usually better than store-bought breads, which tend to be processed and full of sugars and salts. A bite of bread here and there is fine for your pup, but don't make bread a regular part of her diet.

Cashews

A few of these meaty nuts are fine for dogs. Cashews contain antioxidants, proteins, magnesium, and calcium. That said, too many cashews add up in the fat column, and can lead to weight gain in your pup. Cashews make for a different treat once in awhile, but remember to only give your dog unsalted nuts.

Coconut

Coconut is an ideal fruit due to its oil content. Considered a superfood, coconut oil is an anti-inflammatory which can aid in managing skin allergies, arthritis, and inflammatory bowel disorders. Unfortunately, coconut is not a good food option for dogs who have sensitive stomachs or pancreatitis due to the fat content within the coconut meat.

Dates

Dates are not toxic to dogs, and your pup might enjoy the taste of date flesh, but this food is high in sugar and fiber, so only one or two should be fed to a dog at one time. However, the pits' size can be problematic if your dog eats a large amount of them at once; the pits can cause serious bowel obstruction. If possible, pass on the dates as there are better, safer treats out there for your pup.

Mango

Your pup might appreciate strips of mango fruit as a fresh treat. Mango flesh is full of nutritional goodness, including potassium, carotenoids, trace minerals, and vitamins. It can be hard to remove the pit from the mango, and as with some other pitted fruits, this pit contains cyanide. Mango pits can also cause blockages if swallowed whole. If you feed your dog mango, make sure it is cut up and does not include the pit.

Peaches

Like the mango, peaches have nutritional upsides, including Vitamin A which can help your pup fight off infections. Also like the mango, the problem is the peach pit which poses a choking and obstruction hazard and contains cyanide. Cut up any peach that you give to your pup and avoid any part of the pit.

Peanut butter

It's the all-time snack favorite for dogs, and for the most part, its safe for pups everywhere to eat. Peanut butter contains plenty of protein, niacin, Vitamins B and E, and heart-healthy fats. Use raw, unsalted peanut butter only to avoid the chance of giving your dog peanut butter that contains xylitol, an artificial sweetener that is toxic to canines and that is often found in commercial peanut butters.

Yogurt

Yogurt is an acceptable snack for dogs provided it is plain yogurt. Yogurt contains active bacteria that support a healthy digestive system with probiotics. Be aware that some dogs are lactose intolerant and may not digest even plain yogurt easily. Don't feed your dog yogurt that has artificial sweeteners or added sugars; stick with plain yogurt only.

You are now a more educated pet parent who is well on the way to providing the best nutritional life for your four-legged companion. So let's get ready to cook!

Unrecognizable words on any food label are typically something we've learned to stay away from. But there are the good kind, and the bad kind! Google any long words on your dog's food and treat labels. Some will be vitamins- that's the good kind! Others will be chemical, additives, or artificial preservatives—those are the bad kind, and should be avoided!

-Megan Spurrell from NomNomNow-

6

MEALS

The best way to start feeding your adult dog fresh, home cooked meals is to plan out your dog's meals in 2 week segments. Once you develop your own preparation system that matches your schedule, you can branch out to planning more weeks in advance if you so choose.

Remember, your goal is to create wholesome, fresh meals for your dog and know exactly what is going into her food, and therefore, her body. Trust us, your dog will love the foods that you create for her, and you will feel empowered to have such an important role in your dog's current and future health.

We've provided home cooked recipes and a sample 2 week meal plan below to help you get started on this exciting fresh food journey. These plans are highly flexible and adaptable, meaning you can make these meals in any order you choose. Pick any recipe you like from our plan to feed whenever you want. You may even find that your dog has a few favorites, so feel free to feed those meals to her more often than the others.

Give it a go, and don't be discouraged if you have a false start or two. Keep trying and perfecting your craft, and soon your pup will be sitting eagerly in the kitchen waiting for some yummy, tasty meals that you have made for your best four-legged friend. Here's a potential plan that will cover your dog's meals for 2 weeks. Specific recipes can be found below the planner, and we've also provided some more age-specific and medical-specific bonus recipes as well. Let's get this pawty started!

Sample 2 Week Home Cooked Meal Plan

Week 1

Day		Meal 1		Meal 2
Monday	→	Easy-Peasy Turkey & Spinach	→	Woofin' Good Beef Stew
Tuesday	→	Easy-Peasy Turkey & Spinach	→	Woofin' Good Beef Stew
Wednesday	→	Easy-Peasy Turkey & Spinach	→	Woofin' Good Beef Stew
Thursday	→	Waggin' Bean & Beef Crockpot	→	Three Meat Howler Dinner
Friday	→	Waggin' Bean & Beef Crockpot	→	Three Meat Howler Dinner
Saturday	→	Chewy Chicken Crockpot Stew with Apples	→	Savory Salmon & Spinach Dinner
Sunday	→	Chewy Chicken Crockpot Stew with Apples	→	Savory Salmon & Spinach Dinner

Week 2

Day		Meal 1		Meal 2
Monday	→	Chow Down Chili	→	Turkey & Veggie Mutt Mash
Tuesday	→	Chow Down Chili	→	Turkey & Veggie Mutt Mash
Wednesday	→	Mmm, Mmm Minced Chicken, Rice & Vegetable Meal	→	Beefy Mutt Meatloaf
Thursday	→	Mmm, Mmm Minced Chicken, Rice & Vegetable Meal	→	Beefy Mutt Meatloaf
Friday	→	Mmm, Mmm Minced Chicken, Rice & Vegetable Meal	→	Beefy Mutt Meatloaf
Saturday	→	Barkin' Beef & Pork Meal with Veggies & Fruit	→	Pupper Turkey & Pumpkin Pasta
Sunday	→	Barkin' Beef & Pork Meal with Veggies & Fruit	→	Pupper Turkey & Pumpkin Pasta

1. Easy-Peasy Turkey & Spinach Old Standard

This traditional fresh meal is a popular standby for a good reason. It ticks off all the boxes for a simple, hearty meal that packs a nutritional punch your dog is guaranteed to enjoy.

Ingredients:

- 3 pounds of ground turkey
- 1 ½ cups of brown rice
- 3 cups of baby spinach, finely chopped
- 2 carrots, shredded
- 1 zucchini, shredded
- ½ cup of peas, frozen or canned
- 1 tablespoon of olive oil

Directions:

1. In a large pan, add 3 cups of water, then cook the brown rice according to the directions on the package. Set the pan aside.
2. Heat the olive oil in a separate pot.

3. Add the ground turkey to the pot and cook until browned, about 3 - 5 minutes. Be sure to crumble the turkey as it's cooking.

4. Stir in carrots, spinach, zucchini, peas, and brown rice to the pot until the spinach has wilted and the entire mixture is completely cooked through, about 3 - 5 minutes.

5. Let the meal cool completely.

Nutritional Facts per Serving:

Serving size	⟶	1 cup
Calories	⟶	412.3
Calories from Fat	⟶	135.9
Total Fat	⟶	15.1 g
Saturated Fat	⟶	4.2 g
Trans Fat	⟶	0.1 g
Cholesterol	⟶	148.3 mg
Sodium	⟶	152.2 mg
Total Carbohydrate	⟶	31.0 g
Dietary Fiber	⟶	2.5 g
Sugars	⟶	2.1 g
Proteins	⟶	36.1 g

2.   Woofin' Good Beef Stew

Who doesn't love a tasty beef stew? We're willing to bet your dog will roll over for this aromatic, easy to make classic full of veggies and meaty goodness.

Ingredients:

- 1 pound of beef stew meat
- 1 small sweet potato
- ½ cup of diced green beans
- ½ cup of diced carrots
- ½ cup of water
- ½ cup of flour
- 1 tablespoon of vegetable oil

Directions:

1. Cook the sweet potato in the oven or microwave oven (5 - 8 minutes) until it is firm but tender. Set the potato aside.
2. Slice the beef into nickel-sized small chunks.
3. Cook the sliced beef pieces in a pan with a

teaspoon of vegetable oil over medium heat, 10 - 15 minutes or until it's well-done.

4. Take the beef chunks out of the pan and place the drippings in a separate pan.

5. Dice the sweet potato.

6. Heat the beef drippings over medium-low heat.

7. Add flour and water into the drippings and whisk to create gravy.

8. Add the beef pieces, carrots, sweet potato, and green beans into the gravy and stir to coat.

9. Cook the meal until the carrots are tender, about 10 minutes.

10. Let the meal cool.

Nutritional Facts per Serving:

Serving size	⟶	1 cup
Calories	⟶	480
Calories from Fat	⟶	100
Total Fat	⟶	11 g
Saturated Fat	⟶	2 g
Trans Fat	⟶	0 g
Cholesterol	⟶	0 mg
Sodium	⟶	970 mg
Total Carbohydrate	⟶	77 g
Dietary Fiber	⟶	8 g
Sugars	⟶	11 g
Proteins	⟶	18 g

3.   Three-Meat Howler Dinner

Is your dog in the mood for a little bit of everything for dinner? If so, this simple meal which covers all three major meat groups, will have her howling for a second serving.

Ingredients:

- 1 pound of ground beef
- ½ pound of ground turkey
- ½ pound ground chicken
- 1 pound of baby carrots
- 3 cups of brown rice
- 2 small baking potatoes
- 3 eggs, slightly beaten
- 3 cups of low-sodium chicken broth
- 2 cups of water

Directions:

1. In a large, 6-quart pan, cook the ground beef, turkey, and chicken together.

2. Add the brown rice, chicken broth, and water to the meat and cook the ingredients together over medium heat for 30 minutes.

3. After 30 minutes, add the carrots, potatoes, and beaten eggs. Cook for an additional 20 - 30 minutes.

4. Let the meal cool thoroughly.

Please note that the amounts above are for cooking large portions of this meal. It is easy to divide up into storage units and freeze until needed. Let one portion thaw in the refrigerator overnight before serving.

Nutritional Facts per Serving:

Serving size	1 cup
Calories	670
Calories from Fat	280
Total Fat	31 g
Saturated Fat	10 g
Trans Fat	1 g
Cholesterol	380 mg
Sodium	260 mg
Total Carbohydrate	42 g
Dietary Fiber	4 g
Sugars	4 g
Proteins	46 g

4. Chow Down Chili

Chili is a popular meal for people, but can dogs eat it, too? You bet! Don't leave your pup out of the tasty fun. Instead, feed her this super easy to create chili designed just for her.

Ingredients

- 1 pound of ground beef
- 4 carrots
- 1 can of low-sodium or sodium-free tomato paste
- 5 ounces of sodium-free beef broth
- 2 tablespoons of unsalted butter

Directions:

1. Cook the ground beef in a frying pan until browned.
2. Add carrots, tomato paste, and butter to the beef and cook for 5 minutes.
3. Add the beef broth to the mixture.
4. Put the mixture into the oven at 350° and cook for 30 minutes.

Nutritional Facts per Serving:

Serving size	⟶	1 cup
Calories	⟶	660
Calories from Fat	⟶	360
Total Fat	⟶	41 g
Saturated Fat	⟶	17 g
Trans Fat	⟶	2 g
Cholesterol	⟶	170 mg
Sodium	⟶	360 mg
Total Carbohydrate	⟶	28 g
Dietary Fiber	⟶	7 g
Sugars	⟶	17 g
Proteins	⟶	49 g

5. Waggin' Bean and Beef Crockpot Dinner

If you don't have time to stand around and wait for your dog's home made meals to cook, then use this crockpot recipe to do the work for you. Your dog will love the outcome with this beefy, hearty meal.

. . .

Ingredients:

- 2 ½ pounds of ground beef
- 1 ½ cups of brown rice
- 1 15-ounce can of kidney beans
- 1 ½ cup of carrots, chopped
- 1 ½ cup of butternut squash, chopped
- ½ cup of peas, canned or frozen
- 4 cups of water

Directions:

1. Stir the ground beef, carrots, brown rice, kidney beans, peas, squash, and water into a slow cooker.
2. Cover and cook on high heat for 2 - 3 hours or low heat for 5 - 6 hours.
3. Let the food cool completely.

Nutritional Facts per Serving:

Serving size	⟶	1 cup
Calories	⟶	417.9
Calories from Fat	⟶	217.8
Total Fat	⟶	24.2 g
Saturated Fat	⟶	9.8 g
Trans Fat	⟶	0.2 g
Cholesterol	⟶	62.5 mg
Sodium	⟶	171 mg
Total Carbohydrate	⟶	28.9 g
Dietary Fiber	⟶	3.4 g
Sugars	⟶	1.8 g
Proteins	⟶	20.5 g

6. Chewy Chicken Crockpot Stew with Apples

Nothing adds a little fruity zing to stew like some cooked apples. Share this hearty yet fruity meal with your dog, and she will be barking with approval.

. . .

Ingredients:

- 2 ½ - 3 pounds of boneless, skinless chicken breasts and thighs
- 1 small sweet potato, cubed
- 2 carrots, sliced
- 2 cups of peas, frozen
- 2 cups of green beans, frozen
- 1 can of kidney beans, drained and rinsed
- 1 large or 2 medium sized apples, cored and cubed with no seeds
- 2 tbsp of olive oil

Directions:

1. Place the chicken breasts and thighs into a crockpot.
2. Pour enough water into the crockpot to just cover the chicken meat.
3. Add in the carrots, potato, green beans, kidney beans, and apple.
4. Cook the mixture for 8 - 9 hours on low heat.
5. Add the frozen peas to the crockpot and heat for another 30 minutes.
6. Drain the excess water from the crockpot and add in the olive oil.
7. Stir the ingredients with a spatula.
8. Let the food cool.

Nutritional Facts per Serving:

Serving size	⟶	1 cup
Calories	⟶	630
Calories from Fat	⟶	180
Total Fat	⟶	20 g
Saturated Fat	⟶	3 g
Trans Fat	⟶	0 g
Cholesterol	⟶	120 mg
Sodium	⟶	630 mg
Total Carbohydrate	⟶	65 g
Dietary Fiber	⟶	17 g
Sugars	⟶	29 g
Proteins	⟶	53 g

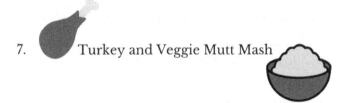

7. Turkey and Veggie Mutt Mash

Lean meat, succulent veggies, and a dash of safflower oil for essential fatty acid goodness are signs that any dog parents will recognize as good for your dog's health. Your pup will just be happy to woof and wolf this tasty meal down.

· · ·

Ingredients:

- 2 pounds of lean ground turkey
- 2 tablespoons for raw turkey or chicken liver, finely pureed or diced
- 2 medium carrots, chopped
- 1 cup of broccoli florets
- 1 cup of cauliflower florets
- ½ zucchini, sliced
- 2 tbsp of olive oil
- 1 tbsp of safflower oil
- 1 ½ cups of water

Directions:

1. Add water to the carrots in a pan. Cover the pan and heat until boiling.
2. Reduce the heat to a low boil and steam until the carrots are tender, about 10 minutes.
3. Place the turkey and raw turkey or liver into a separate skillet. Cook on medium-high heat until it's well-done (no signs of pink). Drain off and discard any fat.
4. Add cauliflower, broccoli, and zucchini to the carrots and cook until all the vegetables are tender, about 6 - 8 minutes.
5. Let the vegetables cool for 5 minutes, then place them in a food processor or chop them with a knife. Aim for a finely chopped consistency.

6. Stir in the chopped vegetables with the turkey and liver.

7. Add olive oil and safflower oil to the mixture.

8. Allow the food to cool completely.

Nutritional Facts per Serving:

Serving size	⟶	1 cup
Calories	⟶	560
Calories from Fat	⟶	310
Total Fat	⟶	35 g
Saturated Fat	⟶	7 g
Trans Fat	⟶	0 g
Cholesterol	⟶	215 mg
Sodium	⟶	270 mg
Total Carbohydrate	⟶	16 g
Dietary Fiber	⟶	7 g
Sugars	⟶	8 g
Proteins	⟶	48 g

8.  Beefy Mutt Meatloaf

This super simple meatloaf recipe for your dog won't take you long to make, and it won't take your dog long to eat it, either! Better yet, this meatloaf might be beefy, but it will keep your dog happy, healthy, and slim.

Ingredients:

- 1 pound of lean ground beef
- 2 eggs
- 1 ½ cups of mixed vegetables (choose your pup's favorites, like broccoli, carrots, and squash)
- 1 ½ cups rolled oats (gluten-free or not)
- ½ cup of cottage cheese

Directions:

1. Preheat the oven to 350°.
2. Mix the beef, eggs, vegetables, rolled oats, and cottage cheese into a bowl until they are thoroughly combined.
3. Press the mixture evenly into a meatloaf pan.
4. Bake for 40 minutes.
5. Let the meal cool.

Nutritional Facts per Serving:

Serving size	⟶	1 cup
Calories	⟶	530
Calories from Fat	⟶	200
Total Fat	⟶	22 g
Saturated Fat	⟶	7 g
Trans Fat	⟶	1 g
Cholesterol	⟶	315 mg
Sodium	⟶	400 mg
Total Carbohydrate	⟶	42 g
Dietary Fiber	⟶	11 g
Sugars	⟶	9 g
Proteins	⟶	39 g

9.   Gobblin' Good Turkey and Rice Meal

It doesn't get much easier than this scrumptious turkey and rice dinner for your dog. This dinner takes no time at all to cook, and it will be well worth it when you see your dog's contented face after eating this meal.

. . .

Ingredients:

- 1 pound of ground turkey
- 2 cups of brown rice
- ½ package of mixed vegetables (or alternatively, choose three of your dog's favorite veggies)
- 1 tsp of rosemary
- 6 cups of water

Directions:

1. Put the ground turkey, rice, rosemary, and water into a large pan.
2. Stir the ground turkey until it is broken up and evenly spread through the mixture.
3. Bring the mixture to a boil over high heat.
4. Reduce the heat to low and let simmer for 20 minutes.
5. Add in the frozen or fresh vegetables. Cook for another 5 minutes.
6. Let the meal cool completely.

Nutritional Facts per Serving:

Serving size	⟶	1 cup
Calories	⟶	530
Calories from Fat	⟶	190
Total Fat	⟶	21 g
Saturated Fat	⟶	6 g
Trans Fat	⟶	0 g
Cholesterol	⟶	125 mg
Sodium	⟶	180 mg
Total Carbohydrate	⟶	50 g
Dietary Fiber	⟶	13 g
Sugars	⟶	9 g
Proteins	⟶	36 g

10.   Mmm, Mmm Minced Chicken, Rice and Vegetable Meal

Here's a quick meal that has all your dog's favorites in a drool-inducing dinner. It's cheap, easy, and tasty, and your dog will love it.

. . .

Ingredients:

- 3 pounds of minced chicken meat
- 4 cups of white rice
- 2 ½ cups of mixed vegetables (frozen and packaged, or pick three or four of your dog's fresh favorites)
- 6 ½ cups of water

Directions:

1. Place the chicken, rice, and vegetables into a large pan.
2. Stir in water until the mixture is smooth in consistency.
3. Put the pan over medium-high heat and bring to a boil. Stir occasionally.
4. Reduce heat to medium-low, cover the pan, and let it simmer for about 25 minutes until all the liquid has been absorbed and the rice is tender.
5. Let the mixture thoroughly cool.

Nutritional Facts per Serving:

Serving size	⟶	1 cup
Calories	⟶	600
Calories from Fat	⟶	70
Total Fat	⟶	8 g
Saturated Fat	⟶	2.5 g
Trans Fat	⟶	0 g
Cholesterol	⟶	235 mg
Sodium	⟶	190 mg
Total Carbohydrate	⟶	54 g
Dietary Fiber	⟶	9 g
Sugars	⟶	7 g
Proteins	⟶	77 g

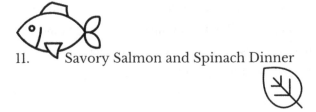

11. Savory Salmon and Spinach Dinner

Change up your pup's meat source with a succulent salmon and spinach meal. Your dog will love the taste, and you'll love knowing that she is getting some seriously nutritious Omega-3 and Omega-6 essential fatty acids.

. . .

Ingredients:

- ½ can of skinless and boneless salmon, drained
- 2 eggs
- ½ cup of frozen spinach, chopped, thawed, and drained
- 1 tsp of extra virgin olive oil

Directions:

1. Heat the olive oil in a nonstick skillet over medium heat.
2. Add the salmon and spinach and cook until heated.
3. Add the eggs and stir until cooked, about 2 minutes.
4. Let the meal cool slightly before serving or freezing.

Nutritional Facts per Serving:

Serving size	1 cup
Calories	390
Calories from Fat	200
Total Fat	23 g
Saturated Fat	6 g
Trans Fat	0 g
Cholesterol	565 mg
Sodium	550 mg
Total Carbohydrate	5 g
Dietary Fiber	5 g
Sugars	2 g
Proteins	42 g

12.   Pupper Turkey and Pumpkin Pasta

Give your dog a nutritious, filling dinner with some pumpkin puree to sweeten the deal. This dinner will look so good when you're done cooking it that you'll want some for yourself!

Ingredients:

- 3 pounds of ground turkey
- 1 cup uncooked whole grain pasta (millet, quinoa, and rice can be substituted if desired)
- 1 carrot, shredded
- 1 squash, shredded
- 1 zucchini, shredded
- 1 apple, chopped with core and seeds removed
- ½ cup pumpkin puree
- ¼ cup unsweetened coconut oil or coconut flakes
- 1 tbsp of olive oil

Directions:

1. Bring 1 cup of pasta to boil in a pot of water. Drain it once it is cooked and tender.
2. Chop and shred the carrot, squash, and zucchini.
3. Cook the olive oil and ground turkey. Drain any excess juices.
4. Heat the vegetables in a separate pan (optional).
5. Combine the vegetables with the ground turkey and pasta.
6. Let food cool completely.

Nutritional Facts per Serving:

Serving size	⟶	1 cup
Calories	⟶	620
Calories from Fat	⟶	270
Total Fat	⟶	30 g
Saturated Fat	⟶	10 g
Trans Fat	⟶	0 g
Cholesterol	⟶	100 mg
Sodium	⟶	95 mg
Total Carbohydrate	⟶	62 g
Dietary Fiber	⟶	12 g
Sugars	⟶	15 g
Proteins	⟶	31 g

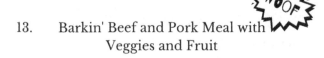

13.   Barkin' Beef and Pork Meal with Veggies and Fruit

Here's a crockpot meal that covers all the nutritional bases for your pup: plenty of meaty protein combined with wholesome fruits and vegetables. Dogs everywhere give four paws up for this recipe!

Ingredients:

- 2 pounds of ground pork
- 2 pounds of ground beef
- 1 large sweet potato
- 2 carrots
- 1 large apple, cored with seeds removed
- 1 cup of rice
- 1 cup of kale
- ½ cup of blueberries
- 1 ½ cups of water

Directions:

1. Place the ground pork and ground beef into a crockpot.

2. Peel and chop the sweet potato, carrots, and apple into 1" pieces.

3. Chop the kale.

4. Mix the fruits and vegetables into the crockpot with the meat.

5. Cook on high heat for 3 - 5 hours or low heat for 5 - 7 hours until the meat is browned.

6. Cook the rice with water in a pan on the stovetop according to the directions on the package.

7. Combine the rice and the crockpot mixture together.

8. Let the meal thoroughly cool.

Nutritional Facts per Serving:

Serving size	⟶	1 cup
Calories	⟶	530
Calories from Fat	⟶	200
Total Fat	⟶	22 g
Saturated Fat	⟶	8 g
Trans Fat	⟶	1 g
Cholesterol	⟶	145 mg
Sodium	⟶	190 mg
Total Carbohydrate	⟶	34 g
Dietary Fiber	⟶	4 g
Sugars	⟶	11 g
Proteins	⟶	48 g

14. Fido's Fish Cake Dinner

For pet parents of dogs who enjoy some seafood in their dinners, this quick fish cake meal is easy to whip together and serve. This recipe is guaranteed to be a winner, winner, fish dinner with your pup!

Ingredients:

- 1 large can of salmon (15 ounces)
- 2 cans of albacore tuna
- 2 large eggs, hardboiled and chopped
- 2 large potatoes, peeled and chopped
- 4 ounces of frozen peas
- 1 large handful of parsley, chopped and divided

Directions:

1. Boil the potatoes in unsalted water until cooked through and tender.
2. Let the potatoes cool, then mash them.
3. Mix ¼" of the parsley in with the potatoes.
4. Cook the frozen peas according to the directions on the packaging.

5. Mix the tuna, salmon, chopped boiled eggs, peas, and remaining parsley in a large bowl.

6. Either add the potatoes to the mixture or serve the potatoes on top of the stacked mixture.

7. Form the mixture into patties appropriate for your dog's size and serve.

Nutritional Facts per Serving:

Serving size	⟶	1 cup
Calories	⟶	650
Calories from Fat	⟶	190
Total Fat	⟶	21 g
Saturated Fat	⟶	6 g
Trans Fat	⟶	0 g
Cholesterol	⟶	590 mg
Sodium	⟶	670 mg
Total Carbohydrate	⟶	46 g
Dietary Fiber	⟶	10 g
Sugars	⟶	15 g
Proteins	⟶	69 g

These 14 recipes can be mixed and matched as you would like and as fits your schedule. It always helps to let your dog chime in on her favorites as well!

Because not all dogs are equal, we've added 5 bones recipes for dogs of certain ages and health situations. Remember, consult with your veterinarian to be sure that these recipes are right for your dog's health.

Chompin' Chicken Casserole for Senior Dogs

Our chicken casserole is chock full of nutritional goodness that your senior dog needs. She will love the meaty flavors and you'll love to see her lick her bowl clean.

Ingredients:

- 4 pieces of boneless chicken with skin
- 1 ½ cups of brown rice
- 1 cup of broccoli
- 1 cup of cabbage
- ½ cup of carrots, peeled and sliced
- ½ cup of spinach
- ½ cup of green beans
- 2 tbsp of olive oil

Directions:

1. Rinse the vegetables, then steam them until they are soft. Set them aside.

2. Put the chicken in a pot, add water to it, and cover. The water should be about an inch above the chicken.

3. Bring the chicken to a slow boil and cook until the meat is cooked for about 20 to 30 minutes. The water should turn into a broth.

4. Remove the chicken from the pot. Keep the broth on hand.

5. Cook the brown rice in three cups of the chicken broth.

6. Remove the chicken skin.

7. Chop the chicken and vegetables into small pieces.

8. Combine the rice, vegetables, chicken, and olive oil into a large bowl. Mix them together and add any remaining chicken broth.

9. Let the casserole cool completely before serving.

Nutritional Facts per Serving:

Serving size	⟶	1 cup
Calories	⟶	560
Calories from Fat	⟶	360
Total Fat	⟶	40 g
Saturated Fat	⟶	9 g
Trans Fat	⟶	0 g
Cholesterol	⟶	60 mg
Sodium	⟶	120 mg
Total Carbohydrate	⟶	39 g
Dietary Fiber	⟶	8 g
Sugars	⟶	7 g
Proteins	⟶	12 g

★ ★ ★

Bonus Recipe 2

Simple Winner Winner Chicken Dinner for Dogs With Skin Allergies

If your dog has a high sensitivity to allergies, she likely suffers from a variety of skin conditions, like hot spots and dry, flaky skin. Here's a recipe that will give your pup only the basics that she needs for nutritional goodness without any extra itch.

Ingredients:

- 2 pounds of boneless, skinless chicken thighs
- 1 cup of spinach
- 1 cup of cabbage, shredded
- 2 eggs
- 1 apple, cored with seeds removed
- 1 tbsp of coconut oil

Directions:

1. Cook the chicken thighs on medium heat in a large skillet.

2. When the chicken is about 75% cooked, add in spinach, cabbage, eggs, apple, and coconut oil.

3. Cover the skillet and let the mixture simmer for 20 minutes.

4. When the chicken is fully cooked, break it up into smaller pieces.

5. Let the food cool completely before serving.

Nutritional Facts per Serving:

Serving size	1 cup
Calories	480
Calories from Fat	170
Total Fat	19 g
Saturated Fat	8 g
Trans Fat	0 g
Cholesterol	360 mg
Sodium	300 mg
Total Carbohydrate	29 g
Dietary Fiber	9 g
Sugars	16 g
Proteins	55 g

★ ★ ★
Bonus Recipe 3

Diabetic Dog Stew

It can be incredibly difficult to make homemade dog food if your dog has diabetes. If your dog is diabetic, this low-glycemic recipe can point you in the right direction to feed your dog a wholesome, healthy meal.

Ingredients:

- 5 pounds of boneless chicken breasts, cut into ½" pieces
- 1 pound of ground turkey
- 4 pounds of chana dal, rinsed
- 2 1-pound bags of brown lentils, rinsed
- 2 1-pound bags of green split peas, rinsed
- 2 1-pound bags of black-eyed peas, rinsed
- 1 pound of pearl barley, rinsed
- 2 16-ounce bags of frozen green beans
- 2 16-ounce bags of frozen crinkle cut carrots
- 2 16-ounce bags of frozen broccoli cuts
- 2 10-ounce packages of frozen spinach
- 1 can (29 ounces) of pure pumpkin

Directions:

1. Put water into a 20-quart pot and bring to a boil over high heat.
2. Add chana dal, black-eyed peas, brown lentils, green split peas, and barley to the water. Reduce to medium heat, stirring occasionally.
3. Cut up and add the chicken breasts to the mixture.
4. Add in the ground turkey.
5. Stir in the pure pumpkin.
6. Add the remaining frozen vegetables to the mixture.
7. Reduce heat to medium-low setting, stirring occasionally until the water is mostly absorbed.
8. Let the food stand and cool thoroughly before serving.

Nutritional Facts per Serving:

Serving size	$\longrightarrow$	1 cup
Calories	$\longrightarrow$	490
Calories from Fat	$\longrightarrow$	60
Total Fat	$\longrightarrow$	7 g
Saturated Fat	$\longrightarrow$	1 g
Trans Fat	$\longrightarrow$	0 g
Cholesterol	$\longrightarrow$	85 mg
Sodium	$\longrightarrow$	220 mg
Total Carbohydrate	$\longrightarrow$	64 g
Dietary Fiber	$\longrightarrow$	20 g
Sugars	$\longrightarrow$	7 g
Proteins	$\longrightarrow$	48 g

★ ★ ★

Bonus Recipe 4

Back on Track Mash for Dogs with Sensitive Stomachs

This recipe is a perfect way to get your dog's digestive system back on track and balanced properly. With a combination of simple, easily digestible ingredients and yogurt with important live cultures to balance gut bacteria, this meal will get your pup feeling back to normal in no time.

. . .

Ingredients:

- 1 plain chicken, boiled with no salt
- ½ cup of canned pure pumpkin
- ½ cup of white rice
- 2 tbsp of plain, unflavored live culture yogurt
- ¼ cup of warm water

Directions:

1. Boil the chicken.
2. Cook the ½ cup of rice according to the package's directions.
3. Mix the canned pumpkin and yogurt into the rice.
4. Tear the chicken up into smaller pieces.
5. Add the chicken to the mixture and stir thoroughly.

Nutritional Facts per Serving:

Serving size	⟶	1 cup
Calories	⟶	310
Calories from Fat	⟶	30
Total Fat	⟶	3.5 g
Saturated Fat	⟶	1 g
Trans Fat	⟶	0 g
Cholesterol	⟶	90 mg
Sodium	⟶	60 mg
Total Carbohydrate	⟶	37 g
Dietary Fiber	⟶	5 g
Sugars	⟶	5 g
Proteins	⟶	33 g

★ ★ ★

Bonus Recipe 5

Sweet Puppy Stew

This stew is easy and quick to cook, so you won't keep your puppy waiting too long for her meal. It's also a great recipe to start off with when you are beginning to home cook for your little pup.

Ingredients:

- 3 pounds of boneless chicken meat
- 2 cups of barley or brown rice

- 6 carrots, peeled and chopped
- 6 large sweet potatoes, peeled and diced
- 1 24-ounce package of frozen peas or lima beans
- 56 fl. ounces of diced tomatoes with juice
- 3 tbsp of oregano or parsley
- ½ cup of fish, olive, or safflower oil
- 1 tsp. iodized salt water

Directions:

1. Place the chicken, rice, carrots, sweet potatoes, peas, tomatoes, parsley, fish oil, and iodized salt water into a stockpot. Add enough water to cover the contents.
2. Bring the ingredients to a boil, then heat to simmer and cover.
3. Cook on simmer for two hours until all the ingredients are soft and most of the water has been absorbed.
4. Let the mixture cool before serving.

Nutritional Facts per Serving:

Serving size	⟶	1 cup
Calories	⟶	550
Calories from Fat	⟶	160
Total Fat	⟶	18 g
Saturated Fat	⟶	4 g
Trans Fat	⟶	0 g
Cholesterol	⟶	155 mg
Sodium	⟶	280 mg
Total Carbohydrate	⟶	64 g
Dietary Fiber	⟶	10 g
Sugars	⟶	15 g
Proteins	⟶	33 g

Let's Get Cooking!

You now have access to 14 easy to create meals for your dog, plus 5 more that may be helpful for you and your pup now or in the future. Of course, meals aren't the only way to pamper and spoil your dog with nutritional goodness. We've got some super tasty recipes for treats in the chapter ahead. Let's get cooking!

Senior dogs need as much protein as younger dogs.

-Megan Spurrell from NomNomNow-

7

TREATS AND COOKIES

There's no better way to end dinner than with some dessert. Tasty treats and cookies don't have to be bad for your dog provided they are made with wholesome ingredients. Treats should only ever be given as such; they should never take the place of your dog's regular meals. Treats are an excellent food reward to use for training purposes, so if you and your dog need to brush up on some sit-and-stays or recall, a homemade treat will make your dog a quick learner.

Everything in moderation is a good standard to live by, and the same goes for your pup. Nonetheless, it's as much fun to watch your pup enjoy a treat as it is to give it to her, so indulge your best four-legged friend with homemade treats made by you with love. Here are a few recipes guaranteed to please your pup!

Treat Recipe #1

Two-Ingredients Tasty Treats

Perfect for novice cooks or for a quick and easy to make treat, these two-ingredients treats are the way to go. Not only are these easy to make, but they are tasty and will have your pup begging for more.

Ingredients:

- 2 cups of 100% organic whole wheat flour (rolled oats, spelt, or wheat germ may be used as a substitute or in combination) *Please note: if you prefer a grain-free version, you can use bean flour, buckwheat, quinoa flour, peanut flour, or coconut flour.*
- 2 (4 ounce) jars of pureed baby food (chicken, blueberry, beef, sweet potato, etc.) *Please note: Make sure that the baby food does not include onions, raisins, or grapes.*

Directions:

1. Preheat the oven to 350 °F.

2. Mix the flour and baby food together to form a stiff dough. Add extra water or flour as needed.

3. Using a lightly floured surface, roll the dough out evenly until it's roughly ¼-inch thick.

4. Use cookie cutters to cut the dough into desired shapes or use a pizza cutter to cut into cubes.

5. Take a cookie sheet and line it with parchment paper. Place the treats about ½-inch apart.

6. Bake the treats for 20 - 25 minutes.

7. Allow the treats to cool completely, then store them in a paper bag. Alternatively, you can store them in an air-tight container, but this will make the treats soft.

Treat Recipe #2

Peanut Butter Bacon Glazed Treats

What does your dog love more than peanut butter? Why, bacon, of course! This recipe combines the best of both worlds and will definitely satisfy your dog's taste buds.

. . .

Ingredients:

Biscuits

- 1 cup of pumpkin
- ½ cup of peanut butter; *Please note: Do not use peanut butter that contains xylitol.*
- 2 eggs
- ¼ cup of canola or coconut oil
- 2 ½ cups of whole wheat flour; *Please note: if you prefer a grain-free version, you can use bean flour, buckwheat, quinoa flour, peanut flour, or coconut flour.*
- 1 teaspoon of baking soda

Glaze

- 2 tablespoons of bacon grease, chicken fat, or coconut oil, melted
- ¼ cup smooth peanut butter; *Please note: Do not use peanut butter that contains xylitol.*

Directions:

1. Preheat the oven to 350 °F.
2. Combine peanut butter, pumpkin, eggs, and oil in a

mixing bowl. Add in whole wheat flour and baking soda.

3. Stir the mixture until a stiff dough is formed. Knead the dough until the flour is fully incorporated.

4. Roll the dough out with a rolling pin and use a dog bone shaped cookie cutter to cut out the shapes, or make little circles like cookies.

5. Bake for 15 minutes.

6. Whisk the peanut butter and bacon grease or coconut oil until smooth. Drizzle over the treats and cool in the fridge or freezer until the glaze hardens.

Treat Recipe #3

Grain Free Apple Peanut Butter Pupcakes

Wouldn't it be great to have a dessert on hand for your dog to have during family celebrations? This easy to make pupcake recipe will look and smell so tasty, you might want to try one too. That's if your dog will share, of course!

. . .

Ingredients:

Pupcakes

- 2 eggs
- 1 apple (any flavor)
- 6 tablespoons of all natural peanut butter; *Please note: Do not use peanut butter that contains xylitol.*
- 1 teaspoon of baking powder

Frosting (optional)

- Pumpkin puree
- Peanut butter (this can be thinned with applesauce if necessary)
- Plain Greek yogurt

"Sprinkles" (optional)

- Frozen or fresh blueberries
- Frozen or fresh peas
- Crushed kibble or dog treats
- Crushed banana chips

Directions:

1. Preheat oven to 350 °F.
2. Finely chop the apple; be sure to remove the core and seeds.
3. Beat the peanut butter and eggs together until smooth. Mix in the chopped apple and baking powder.
4. Take a cupcake tin and line it with cupcake liners. Scoop the mixture into 5 - 6 of the cupcake holes. Fill the holes almost up to the top.
5. Bake the pupcakes for 20 minutes.
6. Remove the pupcakes from the oven and allow them to cool.
7. Optional: Whip up the Greek yogurt with peanut butter and blueberries, or any other combination you choose. Apply the mixture to the top of the cupcakes after they've cooled.

Treat Recipe #4

Summer Blueberry-Pumpkin-Bacon Pupsicles

When you are cooling off with a frozen treat this summer, your dog can enjoy her own treat right alongside you. This recipe is super simple and will definitely keep your dog cool on a hot day.

Ingredients:

- 1 stip of bacon, cooked and crumbled
- 1 can of pumpkin
- Fresh blueberries
- 1 cup of water
- 1 package of thin rawhide strips (for "handles")

Directions:

1. Combine the bacon, pumpkin, and water in a blender and blend until smooth.
2. Place three or four blueberries at the bottom of each popsicle mold.
3. Pour the mixture over the blueberries.
4. Insert one rawhide stick into each mold.
5. Freeze for several hours.

Treat Recipe #5

Homemade Grain Free Breath Freshening Biscuits

With these treats, your dog will have a snack and get fresh breath, too. You'll definitely want to snuggle closer with your pup after she has had one or two of these biscuits. This recipe is a little more involved, but you'll be saving money in the long run by making these biscuits on your own.

Ingredients:

- ½ cup fresh parsley, chopped and packed
- ½ cup fresh mint, packed
- 1 large egg
- 1 tablespoon of diatomaceous earth
- 1 tablespoon of activated charcoal
- ½ teaspoon of grass-fed gelatin
- 2 tablespoons of Brewers Yeast
- 3 tablespoons of organic coconut oil
- 1 tablespoon of ghee, melted
- 1 tablespoon of liquid chlorophyll or freshly juiced wheat grass (optional)
- ½ cup of bone broth or filtered water, warmed
- 4 cups of garbanzo (chickpea) bean flour

Directions:

1. Combine the mint, parsley, charcoal, diatomaceous earth, gelatin, brewers yeast, and egg in a food processor. Process the mixture until smooth.
2. Add melted coconut oil, bone broth, ghee, and chlorophyll, and process it until fully combined into the mixture.
3. Add the garbanzo bean flour ½ cup at a time. Pulse the combination until the mixture resembles dough. The mixture should not be dry; add a few drops of water to moisten it if necessary.
4. Roll the dough out onto parchment paper to about ¼-inch thickness. Cut into desired shapes.
5. Bake at 400 °F for 10 - 15 minutes.
6. Let cool, then store in an air-tight container.

Treat Your Pup Right

Use these recipes to give your dog treats that you know are made with wholesome goodness. Store-bought treats are often made with fillers and processed ingredients, and you want your dog to always eat the best, even when she is having a fun treat. By making your dog's treats yourself, you know that what she is snacking on is good and healthy for her.

Treats are a great way to reward your dog for good behavior between meals. But as part of a healthy diet, they should be a nutritious snack, rather than indulgent treats. Carrots, spinach, kale, cucumbers, bananas, and cantaloupe all make healthy snacks that most dogs love!

-*Megan Spurrell from NomNomNow*-

8

PICKING COMMERCIAL DOG FOOD

Sometimes life gets hectic and you might not have the time necessary to dedicate to cooking for your dog. So what should you do if you need to grab some commercial dog food to tide your pup over until you cook up the next batch of meals? There are so many varieties of dog food on the shelves of pet stores and grocery stores that it can be overwhelming. Which kind is the right one for your dog? Here are some methods to use to help you choose the best commercial food for your dog on the spot.

Reading A Label

Commercial dog food labels can be thoroughly confusing if you're not sure what ingredients to look for and which to avoid. The simplest approach is to keep in mind that the best foods have the highest-quality ingredients. Remember, your dog needs protein, fat, and carbohydrates and the amount she needs is dependent upon her breed, age, health, and activity level.

The items on a dog food label are listed in order by weight, which means that the ingredients list starts with the ingredient used the most and end with the ingredients least used. High-quality foods will list whole proteins first, followed by grains, fruits, vegetables, vitamins, minerals, and essential fatty acids. Foods with labels that list corn, wheat, soy, meat by-products are not quality foods. Avoid feeding your dog commercial foods that contain those ingredients, especially if they are listed first on the label.

Picking The Type Of Food

When you know what to look for on the ingredients label, that should make it easy to choose the best food, right? Not always. Many dry foods, especially the cheaper options, are made to meet only the minimum nutritional standards required by the Association of American Feed Control Officials (AAFCO). Dry food typically incorporates less protein, measured by portion size, than wet or fresh foods. The quality of the proteins will be based on the cost of the food; the more expensive the dry food, the more likely the food contains higher quality meats. Lower-priced foods tend to use chicken by-products or animal meals, which are unhealthy for dogs. Therefore, if you want to choose a good dry food for your dog, you will have to pay more for it.

Dry food is generally affordable and has a lengthy shelf-life, so it lasts much longer than wet or fresh foods. Many commercial dry foods are developed to satisfy basic nutritional requirements for dogs of different ages, sizes, and breeds. When you do select a food, make sure that it includes the following items:

- Whole proteins (chicken, beef, fish, eggs, pork, duck, liver)
- Whole grains (quinoa, brown rice, oats)
- Vegetables (peas, carrots, sweet potatoes)
- Vitamins (A and E)
- Omega-3 and Omega-6 essential fatty acids
- Glucosamine
- Chondroitin

Equally, avoid choosing foods that include these ingredients:

- Poultry by-products
- Animal meal

- Meat by-products
- Corn
- Wheat
- Soy
- Onions
- Garlic
- Propylene Glycol (PG)
- BHA and BHT
- Ethoxyquin

What if you choose to grab some commercial wet food for your dog? You will want to follow many of the same suggestions given for dry foods. It can be tempting to choose wet foods based on how they are pictured on the packaging. Although some wet foods do contain whole meat cuts, just as many have meat meal, meat by-products, and other ingredients that may not be specified. Canned wet foods have "best by" dates on them that you will need to check for valid dates before you purchase any product.

Similarly to dry foods, look for wet foods that have the following characteristics:

- A specific protein source listed first on the label
- Specific sources of animal protein and fat. Look in particular for named muscle tissue and organs
- Vegetables and whole grains
- Limited amounts of grain, vegetables, or meat

byproducts. Ideally, choose a wet food that does not include any of these items, although that may be hard to find.

- A "complete and balanced" label from the AAFCO

The best wet canned foods will include a major protein source, whole and unprocessed grains, and vegetables. If possible, do not give your dog wet food that has by-products, unnamed animal sources, sugar or sweeteners, food binders, preservatives, and artificial colorings.

Remember, your veterinarian can be an invaluable resource to turn to for advice on what commercial foods, both dry and wet, are the best choices for your dog.

In A Pinch

While our book is designed to help you learn to cook homemade food for your dog, we understand that life happens and sometimes, for various reasons, you might not have the time needed to cook meals at home. Use this chapter for guidance when you have to buy commercial food in a pinch for your dog. As soon as you are able, slowly switch your dog back to her normal homemade diet.

If you look at a food or treat and can't tell what's in it, that's already a red flag. If you're told a food will stay fresh in your cabinet or fridge for months (or years) at a time, you should wonder what kind of chemicals are making that possible!

-Megan Spurrell from NomNomNow-

9

MAKING MEALTIME POSITIVE AND SIGNIFICANT

Many pet parents look at mealtime as a means to an end, as opposed to an opportunity to both feed your dog and train her at the same time. Just as people are taught manners when it comes to eating meals, dogs need to be instructed the same way. No, you aren't going to tell your dog not to chew with her mouth open, because that's going to happen anyway, but she should know there are certain rules and protocols to follow before she receives her dinner.

Training your dog during mealtime means that she learns what is expected of her to get dinner, and you retain control over the situation. Using mealtime for training is an excellent way to prevent or eliminate various food-associated behaviors such as begging, speed eating, and food aggression or guarding. First, let's look at the best way to introduce homemade foods to your dog, then we'll look at how to feed her properly.

Introducing A New Food

Dogs are as much creatures of habit as people, and that means it can be tougher than you might think to get your pup to switch from the food she's been eating for awhile to something brand new. Here are some steps to take to help make the transition easier for your dog, and for you!

1. Plan as far ahead as possible.

If you know that you are going to change your dog's food, start planning ahead from the moment you decide to do so. Make sure you have enough of the food your dog is currently eating, preferably at least a week or two's worth,

2. Make a gradual transition.

It's critically important for your dog's digestive system that you make the switch between foods gradually. Mix about 25% of the new food with the current food on the first day, then add a bit more on each subsequent day until your dog is eating 100% new diet.

. . .

3. Stay consistent with feeding times.

Don't change anything about your dog's eating patterns. If you feed her twice a day, continue to do so at the times your normally do. Your pup will be much more comfortable with a change in diet if nothing else about her eating patterns changes. Sudden changes will likely do nothing more than complicate the food switch and frustrate your dog.

4. Mix it up.

If you find that your new homemade food isn't appealing to your dog, don't be afraid to change things up a bit. Add in some warm water or warm gravy to moisten the food and make the smell more attractive to your dog. Remember to discard any food you've added warm water or gravy to after 30 minutes if it remains uneaten to prevent spoilage.

5. Expect a missed meal or two.

Don't be surprised or alarmed if your dog turns her nose up at the new food one or two times, or picks around the new food to eat only the old diet. Missing a couple of meals will not do any damage to your dog's health. However, if she starts missing more than three meals, or refuses to eat at all, it may be necessary to try a different diet altogether. Speak with your veterinarian as well to make sure there are no underlying health problems that may be impacting your dog's appetite.

. . .

6. Observe your pup carefully.

Watch your pup for her response to the new diet. When your dog has accepted the new diet, give it about 6 to 8 weeks to look for examples of how the food is impacting your dog's health. A nutritious, well-balanced diet will support your dog's ideal body condition and weight, promote a healthy coat and skin, and consistent and normal stool levels.

A Proper Introduction To Meals

Although it might seem easier just to fill your dog's food bowl and set it on the floor whenever and wherever, if you want to encourage proper behavior in your dog at meal times, you'll have to be more deliberate in your approach to them. Your dog needs to understand clearly what manners you are trying to teach her. Here are some ways to address some common dog behavioral problems at dinner time.

Basic Meal Time Manners

One of the best ways to teach your dog manners at meal time is to create a strict structure that you don't deviate from at all if possible. It's also an excellent opportunity to teach and practice training fundamentals. By combining training with eating, you'll teach your dog that she has to do some "work" for her food, thereby keeping her focus on you instead of on the food. Try practicing one of these three commands --- or all three, alternately --- with your dog at meal times and watch her manners improve.

Option #1: Teaching the "Sit" Command

1. While you prepare your dog's meal, let her walk freely around you.
2. When you are ready to feed your dog, stand still with the bowl in your hand to get her attention.
3. Call your dog's name and give the command "Sit" while holding the bowl of food slightly above her head. She should look up at you and the bowl and sit back on her haunches.
4. If your dog doesn't sit, but instead moves a step or two backward, then gently press down on her hind

end, holding the bowl up above her head. Again, say your dog's name, then give the command "Sit."

5. When your dog obeys the command, put the food bowl down in front of her. Remember to praise her and allow her to eat the food.

Option #2: Teaching the "Come" Command

1. Have a family member hold your dog on a leash or place her in her crate while you prepare her food.
2. When the meal is prepared, free your dog.
3. Stand with the bowl of food in hand and give the "Come" command.
4. When your dog comes to you, praise her, then set the bowl of food on the ground and let her eat.

Option #3: Teaching the "Wait" Command

1. Have your dog sit at her normal eating spot. Pick up her food bowl in your hand.
2. While she is still sitting, give her the "Wait" command. If she remains seated, say "Yes!" and reward her with a small morsel of food from her bowl. If she breaks out of the seated position, say "Oops!" and put her food bowl back on the counter.

Repeat this step until your dog is holding her sitting position whenever you pick up the bowl.

3. With your dog still in the sitting position, give the command "Wait." Then, lower the food bowl halfway to the ground, about one to two feet from her. If she stays seated, say "Yes!" and give her a small bit of her food. If she gets up, say "Oops!" and raise the bowl up higher over her head. Try again, but don't lower the bowl as much.

4. Keeping your dog in the sitting position, repeat the steps of the "Wait" command until you can place the bowl on the floor without your dog moving. Don't leave her in this position for too long. If she holds still for a couple of seconds, give her an "Okay!" to release her from the "Wait" command. Praise her and let her eat her food.

Any of these three training methods will help your dog to understand that you are her pack leader, and you control the food situation. You are happy to share these yummy meals with her provided she listen to you, focus on you, and do as you ask. Remember to be patient at all stages of these training methods and never use negative or harsh methods to punish your dog in any way. Positive reinforcement, encouragement, and consistency are key to training your dog to have good "table" manners.

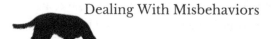

Dealing With Misbehaviors

Food is everything to a dog, so it's no wonder a pup might not think of her training right away when she is instead smelling tempting scents and knows that food is coming soon. At first ,that behavior can seem cute and funny, but once you give your dog permission to behave in a certain way, even subconsciously, it's hard to train that habit out of your dog. Here are some of the most common misbehaviors associated with dogs at mealtime and how you can prevent your dog from acting in these ways or stop her issues altogether.

Begging

It's difficult to turn away from a begging dog. Those big eyes looking up at you, just pleading for one little tidbit of tasty goodness are hard to ignore. Most people don't ignore them, and then they wonder why their dog is constantly in their face while they are trying to eat their own dinner. Begging is one of the most common behavioral issues in dogs at meal-time, and if it isn't nipped in the bud early on, the behavior will escalate. What was originally amusing becomes prob-lematic when your dog is snatching food out of your hand or whining and barking or jumping up in your lap as you try to eat. Here are some steps to address this problem.

Option #1: The "Place" Command

One way to address the begging problem is to teach your dog to go to her "place" outside of the kitchen or dining area. In other words, make sure she knows she is not to be in the room your family is eating in during dinnertime. Create a special place just for your dog, perhaps on a cushy bed or rug, under the living room table, or in her crate. If your dog fails to remain in her "place' after you give her the command and take her to the spot, simply get up and take her there again. Be patient, as you may have to do this repeatedly before your dog understands that she is not going to get table scraps anymore.

Option #2: The Busy Bee Approach

Another means to address your dog's begging issues is to focus her attention elsewhere while you and your family eat. Give your dog her food at the same time your family eats, so she will be too focused on eating her own grub to notice what you're eating. Or, if you eat at a different time from your dog, then give her a chew toy, such as a Kong stuffed with treats, or a puzzle toy where you hide treats for her and she has to work to find them. Your dog will come to associate that time every night as "game time" for her while you get to eat your dinner in peace.

. . .

Option #3: The Buy-In Approach

There's no better way to be sure your message has been received loud and clear than making sure that message is repeated by every party involved; no one is to feed the dog anything but her own food and treats. This approach is the same one that you and all your family members need to take toward your dog's begging habit. The key to preventing and ending begging is consistency. Every member of your family has to be on the same page and follow through together, no matter how often your dog looks at you with big boo-boo eyes (we're looking at you, Dad!). The same rules need to be followed by all visitors, and if you take your dog with you to relatives' or friends' houses, let them know ahead of time the rules you want followed with your pup.

Speed Eating

If your dog likes to wolf her food down at an incredibly fast rate, that's a problem you want to address quickly. A dog who eats her food too fast is likely to overeat or suffer from digestive issues, such as vomiting, after eating. Even worse, your dog is more likely to choke on her food, which is a life-threatening situation. Also, dogs who regularly gulp their food down have a higher chance of developing bloat, or gastric dilatation-volvulus. In this medical condition, the stomach or intestines expand and twist in the abdomen. This deadly condition can quickly cost your dog her life. So if your dog chows down too fast, she's putting her health in danger. Here's how you can help your dog slow down while eating:

Option #1: The Slow Feeder Bowl

There are many brands of slow feeder dog bowls that you can easily find at your local pet store. These bowls tend to have pillars in the middle that force your dog to have to work around them to eat her food, thereby making her slow down.

Option #2: Add a Barrier

You can make it more challenging for your dog to eat her food by placing an object in her bowl that she will have to move around to eat. Choose a flat, smooth stone that is too large for your dog to swallow or use a tennis ball and place it in the middle of your dog's food bowl. She will have to nudge the ball or stone out of the way repeatedly to get to her food, which will automatically slow her down.

Option #3: Puzzle Time

As mentioned in the "Begging" section, there are many doggy brain games and puzzles on the market now. You can place part of your dog's meal in these toys and make her work to get her food. She will have to move or manipulate the puzzle in order to get part of her meal, so she will definitely be eating much more slowly with this tool.

Option #4: Cookies and Muffins

Make it harder for your dog to eat her meal in one gulp by spreading it out over a cookie sheet or within muffin holes in a muffin tray. Either method will force your dog to take small bites and even pick up pieces with her tongue. If you use a muffin pan, just place small parts of her meal in each hole. Your dog will still have to slow down to put her muzzle in every hole to get all the food.

Option #5: Feed by Hand or by Spoon

Offering your dog part of her meal by hand or by spoon will slow down her eating process. If feeding by hand, put some food in your hand, close it, and offer your closed hand to your dog, If she gently licks or noses your hand, open it and give her the food. If your dog uses her teeth on your hand, keep it closed. You can also give your dog scoop of food by spoon, and because she has to concentrate on licking the spoon, she will slow down while eating.

Picky and Reluctant Eaters

What should you do if your dog is a picky eater? If your dog is overly picky or won't eat at all, there is an underlying health issue or behavioral issue to address. If your dog is refusing to eat anything at all --- not even a treat or piece of table scrap --- it's likely a health issue, and you should take your dog to the veterinarian as quickly as possible. In other cases, though, you are probably dealing with a behavioral issue. These are the possible causes of picky eating:

- **Food quality:** Is the food spoiled or rancid? Is your dog used to wet food and now refuses dry food?
- **Boredom:** Has your dog become too attached to table scraps (they taste better than kibble)?
- **Too many treats:** Do you overfeed your dog treats? Treats are typically different in flavor and texture, while main meals are usually the same.
- **Stress:** Are there stressors in your home, like a new pet or a new person? Stress can cause a dog to eat less because she is focused on the changes around her, instead of food.

You can address behavioral issues with your dog in the following ways:

- **Wait it out.** Let your dog go without food for a couple of days. Once she is hungry enough, she will be less picky about what she eats.
- **Cut back on treats.** Put your dog on a "treat diet" and cut back on the amount of treats you feed her per day.

- **Exercise before meals.** Regular exercise can stimulate appetite and improve your dog's metabolism, but give her a short break after the exercise before feeding her.

- **Stick to a schedule and limits.** Feed your dog on a strict schedule, and only leave the food out for 10 minutes. If she doesn't eat it by then, put the food away. Your dog will learn that if she wants to eat, there's a limited opportunity to do so.

- **Switch the feeding location.** Change where your dog eats her meals. Find a spot in your house that is quiet and feed her there. Try to limit any stressors around your dog's mealtime.

- **Rotate the foods.** Switch up the foods your dog gets to decrease the chances of boredom. Try not to switch food types more than once a week.

- **Change the delivery.** Try new dishware or elevated trays. Some dogs, especially seniors, may have trouble accessing food bowls that are low on the ground. For some dogs, a plate instead of a bowl is all they need to chow down on their meals.

If the issue is medical in nature, it may be caused by a wide range of conditions, including dental problems, digestive conditions, injuries, or mental conditions. Again, if you suspect a medical condition that is behind your dog's reluctance to eat, contact your veterinarian right away.

· · ·

Aggression and Food Guarding

Guarding valuable possessions is a natural instinct amongst wild animals, and it's normal behavior in dogs. However, it's not good for domesticated dogs to be exercising this instinct in the home. Food aggression and resource guarding can start out as a relatively harmless behavior and escalate to all-out aggression, with a dog who is biting or chasing a person or other pet away from their food. For many dogs, food is a valuable item, thus they feel the need to guard it, aggressively if need be.

Sometimes food guarding doesn't need to be corrected except by common sense steps: putting the dog in her crate, leaving a dog alone while she is eating, feeding the dog in a separate room. But in cases where guarding becomes dangerous, especially around children, steps must be taken to address the behavior.

If your dog guards her food or shows any signs of aggression at mealtime, there are steps you can take to desensitize and counter-condition her to change this behavior. However, if at any time you are afraid your dog will bite you, stop the training and contact a certified dog behaviorist who can work professionally with you and your pup to get her back on track.

This process is a complex one and takes time, so remember to be patient, consistent, and positive in all your interactions with your dog.

. . .

Stage #1:

1. Have a number of small treats in your pocket before you begin this process. Make sure the treats are high-quality and only use them when you are practicing this training with your dog.
2. Place a bowl of food on the ground and let your dog eat from it. Stand a couple feet away from your dog while she eats. Do not move toward her.
3. Say something conversational, such as, "Say, what have you got there?" At the same time, toss a treat towards the bowl. Do this every few moments until your dog has finished the meal.
4. Repeat this process each time your feed your dog. If she ever steps toward you for more treats, just ignore her. When she does back to the bowl, then begin tossing more treats.
5. Work on this stage until your dog has eaten at least 10 meals in a row in a relaxed manner.

Stage #2:

1. When your dog is eating her food, conversationally state, "Say, what have you got there?" while tossing a treat toward her bowl. At the same time, take one step toward your dog. Then, immediately step back. Repeat this process every few seconds until your dog finishes eating.

2. Every day, take one more step closer to your dog while she eats, then toss a special treat toward the bowl. Continue at this stage until you can step about 2 feet from the bowl. Again, once your dog has eaten 10 meals in a row in this relaxed state, move on to the next stage.

Stage #3:

1. As your dog eats from her food bowl, approach her and say, "What have you got there?" Stand next to the bowl and drop a special treat into it. Then turn around and walk away.
2. Repeat this step every few seconds. When your dog has eaten 10 meals in a row in a relaxed manner, move on to Stage #4.

Stage #4:

1. While your dog eats the food from her bowl, approach her, ask "What have you got there?" and stand next to her with a treat in hand. Bend down slowly and slightly, and hold the treat out just an inch or so in your dog's direction. Encourage your dog to stop eating from the bowl and take the treat. Once she eats the treat from your hand, stand up

and walk away. Repeat this step every few moments until your dog is done eating.

2. Every day, bend down a bit more when you offer the treat so your hand moves an inch or so closer to the bowl. Eventually, you want to hold your hand with the treat right next to the dog's bowl. After your dog has eaten 10 meals in a row in this relaxed fashion, move to the next stage.

Stage #5:

1. When your dog is eating from her bowl, approach her and ask, "What have you got there?" Stand next to your dog, then bend down and touch the bowl with one hand while offering her a treat with the other.

2. Repeat this step every few seconds until your dog is done eating. After she has eaten 10 meals in a row in this manner, move to the next step.

Stage #6:

1. While your dog eats her food from her bowl, walk up to her and ask, "What have you got there?" Stand next to the dog, then bend down and pick up her food bowl. Raise it about 6 inches off the floor

and drop a treat in the bowl. Set it back down immediately so your dog can eat from it again.

2. Repeat the previous step every few minutes until your dog has finished her meal. With each practice session, raise the bowl slightly higher off the floor until you can lift it up to your waist and back.

3. Repeat the sequence again, but this time pick up the dog's bowl and walk to a counter or table with it. Place a treat in the bowl, walk back to your dog, and place the bowl on the floor before her.

Once you have the process down, make sure each member of your family goes through the same training. Do not assume that just because your dog is fine with one person touching her food bowl that she will be good with everyone doing that. The idea here is to make your dog realize that people approaching her food bowl will not take it away; in fact, they will put even tastier treats inside of it!

Always remember to never punish your dog during these training exercises. She is responding to a natural instinct, one that you have to work with. If you do not handle resource guarding the right way, you can severely damage your relationship with your dog. Using these desensitization techniques is by far the better and safer way to go.

Time To Chow Down!

In this chapter, we've covered many of the trouble spots you can encounter when teaching your dog basic eating manners. Stay positive, consistent, and engaged when training your dog and she will return your enthusiasm and love. If at any point you feel over your head, contact a dog trainer or animal behaviorist for assistance. Reach out to your veterinarian as well if you think your dog has medical issues that need to be diagnosed and addressed. Otherwise, you should have a happy dog who knows the ground rules for eating in the house and who is ready to dig into some of that tasty homemade food you've made just for her.

A Dog's sense of smell is 10,000 – 100,000 times more acute as that of humans.

-PBS-

AFTERWORD

Remember that person who started reading this book a short while ago, the one who wasn't sure where to begin when it came to cooking homemade meals for their dog? Yes, that's right: you! Now you're armed with a wealth of practical knowledge about dog nutrition as well as several simple, quick recipes to keep your dog's stomach full and tail wagging for the rest of her life.

As a quick review, here are the main points and information you've learned from our text, followed by the appropriate chapter number for you to return to for a more in-depth examination.

First, remember why you've decided to take this journey in the first place: your belief that your dog deserves a better, more wholesome and nutritious diet for her current and future health. Unfortunately, when you buy commercial foods for your pets, you have no control over what is included in the food. By cooking your dog's meals yourself, you know every ingredient that makes its way into that bowl. There's no more guessing or hoping that the commercial food you've purchased is "good enough" for your pup. It's also important to recall that feeding your dog nutritious food means that she will have a stronger immune system that will better fight off illnesses as she ages. Some commercial foods may actually be responsible for long-term health problems in dogs, so deciding to switch to a fresh food diet shows how much your dog means to you and your life. (see Chapter 1: Why Dog Nutrition Matters)

A homemade diet is nutritionally superior to commercial dry and wet foods. Fresh food diets lead to more energy, healthier skin and coat, better digestion, and a better quality of life. Switching your dog to a new food requires patience and time, so discuss the change with your veterinarian to obtain their input before you start feeding the new food to your pup.

The basic makeup of a dog's nutrition is always important to keep in mind as you create and cook meals for her. Proteins, carbohydrates, fats, fiber, vitamins, minerals, and water are all necessary for a complete canine diet. How much of each component varies according to a dog's age, breed, size, and health. A conversation with your veterinarian will help you determine the exact percentages of each ingredient your dog needs in her food. (Chapter 2: Nutrients in a Dog's Diet)

When you are creating your dog's meals, remember the ingredients you need to include to keep her food appropriately balanced. You will want to craft meals that include muscle meat, liver and kidney, dairy products, eggs, vegetables, fruit, and grains. Then, we discussed proper food portions and making sure that your dog doesn't overeat to prevent behavioral issues and future health problems. Creating a feeding schedule for your dog is almost as important as making the food in the first place. Use our easy guide to create your own schedule using your personal availability. (Chapter 3: Perfect Portion Sizes)

If you are raising a puppy, special care and attention need to be applied to a puppy's diet. Growth tends to happen quickly with puppies, and they need the right balance of nutrients, vitamins, and minerals to grow to their full puppy potential. Because puppies grow at such a substantial rate within the first year of life, you want your puppy to receive the nutrition she needs to go full steam ahead into adulthood. Use our puppy feeding chart and balanced nutrition chart to help you develop a puppy power plan for your dog. (Chapter 4: Feeding Growing Puppies)

Of course, just as there are foods dogs should eat, there are also foods they should avoid. Nuts, alcohol, chocolate, grapes, and raisins are just a few of the foods that can be problematic and sometimes life-threatening for dogs. There are even some foods that should be given to dogs only with great caution. Review this chapter and make sure that these ingredients are never in your dog's diet. If you must have these items in your house, keep them out of your dog's reach. (Chapter 5: Foods to Avoid and Foods to Approach With Caution)

We have provided 19 homemade dog food recipes for you complete with ingredients and instructions to give you the confidence to begin feeding your dog a new diet. Follow our sample two-week feeding schedule if you so choose, or change it up as you see fit to best meet the needs of you and your dog. These quick and simple meals will make it easy for your dog and you to make the switch to a nutritious fresh food diet. (Chapter 6: Meals)

What's a meal without a dessert to end the evening? And for dogs, desserts equal treats! Just as you've now learned to create nutritious meals where you control the ingredients, you can now do the same for your dog's biscuits. Don't feel guilty about giving your dog treats anymore. What you'll be cooking up for your pup is natural goodness, and given in moderation, your puppy will never know that what she's eating is actually pretty good for her! (Chapter 7: Treats and Cookies)

We've included a chapter on commercial dog food because sometimes you might find yourself in a bind and need to grab some food from the store for your dog. In this chapter, we go over what to look for to choose the best commercial food possible to hold you over until you get a new batch of food cooked up. Choose a substitute food using our guide and your veterinarian's input. (Chapter 8: Picking Commercial Dog Food)

Once you've got your menu and meals together, it's time to address any behavioral issues your dog may exhibit come mealtime. Starting with a regular schedule and gradual switching from old to new food, you can set the tone for what dinner time will be for your pup. Whether your dog begs, gulps food, or is protective or aggressive around her food, you can use mealtime to train your dog to behave appropriately before she gets her bowl of tasty goodness. Follow our training suggestions, and you'll have a well-behaved dog every time you and your family sits down to eat. (Chapter 9: Making Mealtime Positive and Significant)

Pawsitively Delicious Meals

Now you've got all the information you need to give your dog the food her body needs most. That's the sign of an incredibly loving and dedicated pet parent. Your dog might not be able to say in words how much she will appreciate your actions, but she will definitely let you know come mealtime! Thank you for reading our book, and we hope that you will give homemade cooking for your dog a try so you can have a healthy, happy dog with an excellent quality of life for many years to come. Enjoy cooking for your pup, and "bone appetit"!

THANK YOU

Thank you for reading this book and allowing us to share our knowledge of this fascinating breed with you.

For more information and to keep up with us follow our publisher:

- Facebook: facebook.com/admorepublishing
- Instagram: instagram.com/admore.publishing
- Youtube: Admore Publishing

If you enjoyed reading this book, please leave us a review! It will help us spread more of our content and create a better relationship between owners and their dogs!

Thank you.

Sincerly,

The Woof Brothers

RESOURCES

Besides our own knowledge and experiences, I used the following awesome sources to create this book:

AKC Staff. (2019, May 29). Foods Your Dog Should Never Eat. Retrieved from https://www.akc.org/expert-advice/nutrition/human-foods-dogs-can-and-cant-eat/

ASPCA. (2015, September 29). Animal Poison Control Alert: The Dangers of Moldy Food. Retrieved from https://www.aspca.org/news/animal-poison-control-alert-dangers-moldy-food

ASPCA. (2019). Food Guarding. Retrieved from https://www.aspca.org/pet-care/dog-care/common-dog-behavior-issues/food-guarding

Battersea Dogs and Cats Home. (2019, July 23). Toxic food for dogs. Retrieved from https://www.battersea.org.uk/pet-advice/dog-care-advice/toxic-food-dogs

Becotte, J. (2018, August 21). Homemade Diabetic Dog Food Recipe - Ruby Stewbie. Retrieved from https://myuntangledlife.com/homemade-dog-food-for-diabetic-dogs/

Bender, A. (2019, January 27). Learn How to Train Your Dog to Stop Begging. Retrieved from https://www.thesprucepets.com/train-a-dog-to-stop-begging-1117892

Brady, C. How Much Should I Feed my dog? Retrieved from https://dogsfirst.ie/raw-faq/how-much-should-i-feed-my-dog/

Brita. (2018, April 24). Dog Dinner Recipe: Fish Cakes. Retrieved from https://foodwithfeeling.com/dog-dinner-recipe-fish-cakes/

Central Garden & Pet. (2018). Dog Training 101 - 4 Phases to Building an Unbreakable Bond with Your Dog. Retrieved from https://www.avodermnatural.com/blog/dog-training-101-best-bond

Daisy the French Bulldog. (2015, June 2). Tasty Tuesday: Pumpkin-Blueberry-Bacon Pupsicles. Retrieved from http://daisythefrenchbulldog.blogspot.com/2015/06/tayuday-pumpkin-blueberry-bacon.html

Damn Delicious. (2018, June 7). DIY Homemade Dog Food. Retrieved from https://damndelicious.net/2015/04/27/diy-homemade-dog-food/

Damn Delicious. (2018, February 5). Easy Crockpot Dog

Food. Retrieved from https://damndelicious.net/2015/05/13/easy-crockpot-dog-food/

Dog Food Insider. (2016, September 21). 6 Tips For Introducing Your Dog To A New Dog Food. Retrieved from https://www.dogfoodinsider.com/6-tips-introducing-dog-new-dog-food/

Dogster HQ. (2019, May 13). Dog Feeding Schedule: How Many Times a Day Should I Feed My Dog? Retrieved from https://www.dogster.com/dog-food/dog-feeding-schedule

Dyck, A. (2015, December 8). The Best Kind of Protein for Dogs. Retrieved from https://blog.homesalive.ca/the-best-kind-of-protein-for-dogs

Elliott, P. (2019, April 25). Which Fruits are Safe for Dogs to Eat? Discover the Benefits & Pitfalls. Retrieved from https://petcube.com/blog/dog-fruits/

Emily's Homestead. (2016, August 18). Homemade Dog Food. Retrieved from https://emilyslittlehomestead.com/2014/01/17/homemade-dog-food/

Finlay, K. (2017, March 29). How to Get Your Dog to Eat More Slowly. Retrieved from https://www.akc.org/expert-advice/health/4-ways-to-slow-your-dogs-eating/

Fleming, A.-M. (2018, September 11). Our Favorite Homemade Dog Food Recipes for Senior Dogs. Retrieved from https://dogquality.com/blogs/senior-dog-blog/our-favorite-homemade-dog-food-recipes-for-senior-dogs

Flowers, A. (2018, June 14). Dog Nutrition: Essential Nutrients for Health and Feeding Basics. Retrieved from https://pets.webmd.com/dogs/dog-nutrition#1

Fitbark. (2018, January 8). How to Pick the Best Dog Food. Retrieved from https://www.fitbark.com/blog/how-to-pick-the-best-dog-food/

Golani, T. (2019, July 22). 33 Best Homemade Dog Food Recipes that are Vet Approved. Retrieved from https://www.favorablethings.com/33-best-homemade-dog-food-recipes-that-are-vet-approved/

Goodall, C. (2015, March 27). Dog Food Recipes: Puppy Stew. Retrieved from https://thebark.com/content/dog-food-recipes-puppy-stew

Goodall, C. (2016, August 5). 3 Ways to Make a Healing Mash for Dogs with Diarrhea & Gas. Retrieved from https://everydayroots.com/healing-mash-for-dogs

Hill's Pet Nutrition. (2019). Fatty Acid Benefits in Dog's Health: Hill's Pet. Retrieved from https://www.hillspet.com/dog-care/nutrition-feeding/fatty-acids-for-dogs

Jones, S. (2019, May 21). Kiss Kibble Goodbye: Homemade Dog Food Recipes. Retrieved from https://www.caninejournal.com/homemade-dog-food-recipes/

Kanaka, R. (2017, March 31). Top 20 healthy homemade dog food recipes your dog will love. Retrieved from https://www.thedogbakery.com/blogs/news/top-20-healthy-homemade-dog-food-recipes-your-dog-will-love

Kimball, C. (2012, October 25). DOG-I-Y: Easy Two-Ingredient Homemade Dog Treats. Retrieved from https://dog-milk.com/doggiy-easy-two-ingredient-homemade-dog-treats/

Laverdure-Dunetz, D. (2018, November 19). Let's Talk Dog Nutrition - 6 Essential Nutrients Dogs Need. Retrieved from https://www.dogster.com/dog-food/dog-nutrition-nutrients-dogs-need

Leicester, D. (2018, November 7). 13 Human Foods That Are Dangerous For Dogs: What Can't Dogs Eat? Retrieved from https://www.vets-now.com/2017/01/foods-poisonous-to-dogs/

Leonardi, L., & . (2013, July 17). Making Homemade Puppy Food. Retrieved from https://www.petcarerx.com/article/making-homemade-puppy-food/1224

Lindsay. (2018, September 18). Homemade Dog Treats. Retrieved from https://pinchofyum.com/homemade-dog-treats

Loveitt, J. (2018, February 21). Added Salt In Dog Food - Should You Be Worried? - PetFoodReviewer. Retrieved from https://petfoodreviewer.com/added-salt-dog-food/

LUVSNOW17. (2007, April 13). Lucky and Rippy's Favorite Dog Food Recipe. Retrieved from https://www.allrecipes.com/recipe/139453/lucky-and-rippys-favorite-dog-food/

Massey, D. (2018, May 7). Vitamins and minerals required in dog nutrition. Retrieved from https://www.nomnomnow.com/blog/vitamins-and-minerals-required-in-dog-nutrition

Mikaela. (2018, January 3). Grain Free Apple Peanut Butter Pupcakes. Retrieved from http://www.wyldflour.com/grain-free-apple-peanut-butter-pupcakes

Miller, P. (2019, April 22). Utilize Feeding Time as Training Time. Retrieved from https://www.whole-dog-journal.com/training/utilize-feeding-time-as-training-time/

Nielsen, M. (2018, June 28). Ingredients You Shouldn't Feed Your Pooch. Retrieved from

https://blog.healthypets.com/informative/bad-dog-food-ingredients-aware/

NomNomNow. The Definitive Guide to How Much You Should Feed a Puppy. Retrieved from https://www.nomnomnow.com/puppy-feeding-guide#importance-of-proper-puppy-nutrition

NomNomNow. (2018). Dog Food Nutrients and Ingredient Quality. Retrieved from https://www.nomnomnow.com/learn/pet-food-information/dog-food-nutrients-and-ingredient-quality

NomNomNow. (2018). Dog Won't Eat. Retrieved from https://www.nomnomnow.com/dog-not-eating

NomNomNow. What Is NomNomNutrient Mix? Retrieved from https://www.nomnomnow.com/learn/pet-expert/what-is-nomnomnutrient-mix

Palika, L. (2016, September 26). Teaching Your Dog Good Food Manners. Retrieved from https://www.

thehonestkitchen.com/blog/teaching-your-dog-good-food-manners/

Peña, M. (2017, July 31). Can Dogs Eat Potatoes Safely? What About Sweet Potatoes? Retrieved from https://www.dogster.com/lifestyle/can-dogs-eat-potatoes-sweet-potato

Pet Poison Hotline. (2019). Bread Dough Toxicity in Dogs and Cats. Retrieved from https://www.petpoisonhelpline.com/poison/bread-dough/

Quach, C. (2018, April 10). The Most Dangerous Human Foods for Dogs. Retrieved from https://www.nomnomnow.com/blog/dangerous-human-foods-for-dogs

Randall, S. (2018, July 1). Recipe: Homemade Dog Food for Sensitive Skin. Retrieved from https://topdogtips.com/homemade-dog-food-for-sensitive-skin/

redgirl. (2008, May 4). Homemade Dog Food Recipe. Retrieved from https://www.allrecipes.com/recipe/140286/homemade-dog-food/

Ringo, A. (2018, December 19). Can Dogs Eat Walnuts?: Cuteness. Retrieved from https://www.cuteness.com/13707559/can-dogs-eat-walnuts

Riviera, C. (2018, September 10). High Fiber Dog Food: Reasons, Types, & Tips. Retrieved from https://www.honestpaws.com/blogs/pet-care/high-fiber-dog-food

Ryczek, H. (2018, November 15). Breath Freshening Dog Treats {Homemade Grain-Free Greenies}. Retrieved from

https://www.healthstartsinthekitchen.com/2015/12/10/
homemade-greenies-breath-freshening-dog-treats/

Star, N. (2018, April 25). DIY: Healthy Homemade Dog Food.
Retrieved from http://wheresthefrenchie.com/diy-healthy-
homemade-dog-food/

Straus, M. (2019, July 6). Homemade Cooked Diets for Dogs.
Retrieved   from   http://dogaware.com/articles/
wdjhomemade3.html#amounts

Stregowski, J. (2019, July 5). Preparing Homemade Puppy
Food. Retrieved from https://www.thesprucepets.com/
homemade-puppy-food-4174007

Tokic, A. (2019, March 5). Beefaloaf Meatloaf Dog Food
Recipe. Retrieved from https://www.petguide.com/health/
dog/beefaloaf-meatloaf-dog-food-recipe/

U. S. F. and D. A. (2019, June 27). FDA Investigates Potential
Link Between Diet & Heart Disease in Dogs. Retrieved from
https://www.fda.gov/animal-veterinary/news-events/fda-
investigation-potential-link-between-certain-diets-and-
canine-dilated-cardiomyopathy

Weldon, L. G. (2017, April 12). Why You Should Make
Healthy Homemade Dog Treats. Retrieved from https://
goodmenproject.com/guy-talk/make-healthy-homemade-
dog-treats-bbab/

Whole Dog Journal. (2019, August 1). Buying the Best
Canned Dog Food: The NEW Approved Wet Dog Food List
is Here! Retrieved from https://www.whole-dog-journal.

com/food/buying-the-best-canned-dog-food-the-new-
approved-wet-dog-food-list-is-here/

Zeltzman, P. (2015, August 27). 7 Reasons Why Dog Obesity
is Dangerous. Retrieved from http://www.pethealthnetwork.
com/dog-health/dog-diet-nutrition/7-reasons-why-dog-
obesity-dangerous